Su**g**
LOVE
SIGNS

PISCES
19 FEBRUARY–19 MARCH

by Jacqui Deevoy

Your heavenly guide to
LIFE, LOVE and BOYS

It's cosmic!

mustard

First published in 1999 by Mustard

Mustard is an imprint of Parragon

Parragon
Queen Street House
4 Queen Street
Bath BA1 1HE
UK

Produced by Magpie Books, an imprint of
Robinson Publishing Ltd, London

Page design by Sandie Boccacci

ISBN 1-84164-189-8

A copy of the British Library Cataloguing-in-Publication Data is
available from the British Library

Printed and bound in the EC

Contents

Part 10: YOUR YEAR AHEAD: THE YEAR 2000 AT A GLANCE

Part 11: INTO THE NEW MILLENNIUM!

Part 12: BIRTHDAY CHART

For all my favourite Pisceans:

Roz
Chris
Georgia
Michael
Lesley
Sarah
Rebecca
Rachael
Karen

Part 1:
All About
Pisces

# A Brief Introduction To Your Sign . . .

Pisces is the twelfth (and last) sign of the zodiac and is concerned with love, dreams, magic, poetry, memories, humour and secrets. Ruled by gentle Neptune, you come across as serene, dreamy, caring, creative and romantic. It's Uranus you have to thank for any psychic abilities you might have and for your out-of-this-world aura! Before Neptune was discovered, Pisces was ruled by Jupiter and this jolly planet still has an effect on you in that it makes you optimistic, broad-minded and extremely kind and generous. Your best qualities are your willingness to help others, your creativity, your compassion and your belief in the power of love. But there's another, not so positive, side to your personality. . . You're sometimes accused of being gullible, sorry for yourself, moody, woolly-headed and depressing. (Oh dear. . .) You also have a tendency to blame others for any bad luck or unhappiness you might experience, refusing to take responsibility for it yourself.

Generally, though, the overall impression you give is of an extremely considerate, charitable and clever person – someone who's talented and clever, yet amazingly modest.

As a small child, you were a real little sweetie – all

dimples and smiles. You were highly imaginative, but may have lived in a make-believe world all of your own. In fact, as a Piscean child, you were more likely than most to have an imaginary friend.

These days, you're still dimply and smiley and your imagination remains fertile, but your tendency to take the worries of the world on your shoulders can sometimes make you self-pitying and this, in turn, can lead to the most spectacular temper tantrums, during which you swing from elation to despair in a matter of seconds. (The imaginary friend has gone though – if that's any consolation!)

The biggest problem you face is your low self-esteem: this can really get in the way of you getting on, and can stop you from making and keeping friends. You also find it hard to face facts sometimes and, when something horrible's happening, you'd much rather stick your head in the sand and pretend you haven't noticed it than deal with it in a mature and responsible way.

The aspect of your personality that most people admire is your ability to be sympathetic to friends and strangers alike. And your casual, laid-back and almost fatalistic approach to life is often envied, especially by those who have a desperate need to be in control.

Here you are in a nutshell:

You're great . . . because you're friendly, caring and considerate.

You grate . . . because you say one thing and think

another, you don't stick up for yourself enough and you've got your head permanently stuck where the sun don't shine!

You rate . . . the sea and anything ocean-connected, romance and privacy.

You hate . . . people in positions of authority, being told to "get a grip", excessive noise and crowds.

You're late . . . with alarming regularity. (Even Pisceans *with* watches – and *they*'re few and far between – are unlikely to have watches that actually work!)

As a mate . . . occasionally you seem a bit insecure but you're understanding and loyal.

As a date . . . you can come over as a bit wishy-washy but you're keen to please and adaptable.

Your fate: To learn the meaning of inner peace.

Lucky Stuff

Numbers: 6 for Pisces; 3 for Neptune – your ruling planet.

Day: Thursday.

Colours: Sea green, violet, pale blue and soft pink. Wear these shades at every opportunity and they'll bring you luck.

Gemstones: Emeralds and sapphires for Pisces; coral for Neptune. And, because you're a Water sign, moonstones, pearls and aquamarines are also said to be very lucky for Pisceans.

Metal: Tin.

Flowers: Carnations, poppies, honeysuckle and all water plants, especially water-lilies. Pretty, decorative and delicate – much like you!

Food: Anything watery – melons, cabbage, cucumber, mushrooms and lettuce to name but a few. Oh and try pumpkin pie – you'll love it!

Animals: Fish, dolphin, sheep and ox. Most Pisceans can liken themselves to at least one of these beasts: which one do you identify with?

Bird: Swan. Beautiful in a kinda spooky way; gentle most of the time, but quite vicious when riled. Ring any bells, Miss Pisces?

Cities: Alexandria, Bournemouth and Seville. If you're a Piscean living in one of these cities already, count yourself *extra* lucky!

Your Rising Sign = The You Others See

In astrology, if you want to discover more about your outer personality and how you come across to others, it helps if you know your Ascendant. Working it out can be a problem, but using the specially devised chart over the page, it couldn't be easier. So look yourself up . . .

A Bit About Rising Signs

Your Rising Sign is the main indicator of your outer personality (i.e. how others see you as opposed to how you view yourself) and also has a major bearing on the way you look and the impact you make on the opposite sex. When combined with your Sun Sign, you'll get an even more accurate picture.

It's important to take British Summer Time into account when working out your Rising Sign. This period varies from year to year but, to keep things simple, if you were born between March 16 and October 31 of any year, subtract one hour from your time of birth. If you were born between midnight and 1 a.m. during the Summer Time period, your birth hour will be 11 p.m. or 12 midnight on the previous day. If you're uncertain about your birth time, all you can do is read through all twelve descriptions on the following pages and see if you can spot yourself. It shouldn't be difficult.

Born abroad? Well, find out the time difference between the United Kingdom and your place of birth. If you were born in a country that is ahead of the UK time-wise, then subtract the number of hours' difference from your birth time; if you were born in a country that's behind the UK time-wise, then add that number of hours to your birth time.

How To Use The Rising Signs Chart

1. Locate your birth date in the first (left-hand) column on the chart on pages 8 and 9.

2. Find your birth hour along the top of the page. If you were born between hours, work it out to the nearest hour. For example, if you were born at 8.45 a.m., your birth hour is 9 a.m. If you were born at 6.20 p.m., your birth hour is 6 p.m. If you were born at exactly half past the hour, go to the next hour (i.e. being born at 4.30 a.m. would give you the birth hour of 5 a.m.) Don't forget to subtract an hour if you were born between March 16 and October 31.

3. At the point where the two columns meet, you'll find an astrological symbol. Look up this symbol in the Symbol Index on page 10 and find out what your Rising Sign is.

4. Then turn the page, find your Rising Sign and discover more about the way others – blokes included! – perceive you. **Note:** If the description doesn't sound like you, check the sign before and after. Because the chart is general, 100 per cent accuracy is impossible for everyone who uses it, and some people may, by the skin of their teeth, fall into the wrong category.

RISING SIGNS CHART

TIME ▶ DATE ▼	1 AM	2 AM	3 AM	4 AM	5 AM	6 AM	7 AM	8 AM	9 AM	10 AM
Jan 1–16	♎	♏	♏	♏	♐	♐	♑	♑	♒	♓
Jan 17–Feb 21	♏	♏	♐	♐	♑	♑	♑	♒	♓	♈
Feb 22–Mar 29	♐	♑	♑	♒	♒	♓	♈	♉	♉	♊
Mar 30–Apr 29	♑	♒	♓	♓	♈	♉	♊	♊	♋	
Apr 30–May 19	♒	♓	♈	♈	♉	♊	♊	♋	♋	♌
May 20–Jun 8	♓	♈	♉	♊	♊	♋	♋	♌	♌	
Jun 9–24	♈	♉	♊	♊	♋	♋	♋	♌	♌	♍
Jun 25–Jul 17	♉	♊	♊	♋	♋	♌	♌	♌	♍	♍
Jul 18–Aug 14	♊	♊	♋	♋	♌	♌	♍	♍	♍	♎
Aug 15–Sep 19	♋	♋	♌	♌	♌	♍	♍	♎	♎	♎
Sep 20–Oct 29	♌	♌	♍	♍	♎	♎	♎	♏	♏	♐
Oct 30–Dec 8	♍	♍	♍	♎	♎	♏	♏	♏	♐	♐
Dec 9–31	♎	♎	♏	♏	♐	♐	♐	♑	♑	♒

11 AM	12 NOON	1 PM	2 PM	3 PM	4 PM	5 PM	6 PM	7 PM	8 PM	9 PM	10 PM	11 PM	12 M'NT
♓	♈	♉	♊	♊	♋	♋	♌	♌	♌	♍	♍	♎	♎
♈	♉	♊	♊	♋	♋	♌	♌	♍	♍	♎	♎	♎	♏
♊	♋	♋	♌	♌	♍	♍	♍	♎	♎	♎	♏	♏	♐
♋	♌	♌	♍	♍	♍	♎	♎	♏	♏	♏	♐	♐	♑
♌	♌	♍	♍	♎	♎	♎	♏	♏	♐	♐	♐	♑	♑
♍	♍	♍	♎	♎	♏	♏	♏	♐	♐	♑	♑	♒	♓
♍	♍	♎	♎	♏	♏	♏	♐	♐	♑	♑	♒	♒	♓
♎	♎	♎	♏	♏	♐	♐	♐	♑	♑	♒	♓	♈	♉
♎	♎	♏	♏	♐	♐	♑	♑	♒	♒	♓	♈	♉	♉
♏	♏	♐	♐	♐	♑	♑	♒	♓	♈	♉	♉	♊	♊
♐	♐	♑	♑	♒	♓	♈	♉	♉	♊	♊	♋	♋	♌
♑	♑	♒	♓	♓	♈	♉	♊	♊	♋	♋	♋	♌	♌
♒	♓	♈	♉	♊	♊	♋	♋	♌	♌	♌	♍	♍	♎

Symbol Index

♈ Aries
♉ Taurus
♊ Gemini
♋ Cancer
♌ Leo
♍ Virgo
♎ Libra
♏ Scorpio
♐ Sagittarius
♑ Capricorn
♒ Aquarius
♓ Pisces

If your Rising Sign is ARIES (♈), you're striking looking, with bold (though not necessarily even) features, a bony angular face and fine hair. Most females with Aries Rising are of average height, but because of their "big" personalities, they often come across as taller. Aries rules the head and this could be why you're so often described as headstrong. Others see you as dynamic, assertive and impulsive, and you tend to attract people who are just as lively as you. The Aries motto is "I am" and you can come across as rather self-centred. But it can also make you appear confident and focused – both very attractive qualities. Boys love you but are sometimes put off by your forcefulness. If they are, then they're the ones who are going to lose out . . .

If your Rising Sign is TAURUS (♉), your personality is as strong and solid as your body. Females with Taurus Rising tend to be short to medium height, but make up for any lack of stature with amazing strength. You can recognize a Taurus Rising type by her square face and thick curly – usually dark – hair. Taurus rules the throat and neck and this may be why you have such a sexy and seductive voice. What people like most about you is the fact you're so down-to-earth and trustworthy – that's the way they see you anyway. The Taurus motto is "I have" and this way of thinking can cause you to be rather possessive. Unless you can curb this part of your personality – and it needs restraining because it shows itself almost as soon as you meet somebody – it could be off-putting, especially when you're trying to pull. When it comes to love, you can be a bit shy, but once you find a bloke who makes you feel secure and sexy, you'll relax and let it all hang out.

If your Rising Sign is GEMINI (♊), you're fast in every way – light on your feet, quick-thinking and an incessant chatterer – and this gives an impression of you being younger than you are. Girls with Gemini Rising tend to be medium height and very slim. You may be a tad flat-chested but you're by no means boyish – you're all woman and proud of it! You've got a cheeky expression with sparkling eyes and long arms and legs (the parts of the body ruled by Gemini). You're always on the go and never seem to finish one project before starting another. You reckon this is due to your flea-like concentration span, but other people think it's down to the fact that you're multi-talented! The Gemini motto is "I talk" and while this can be attractive to some people, it can put others right off, especially when your mouth runs away with you. Boys find you irresistible – once you learn to talk less and listen more you're bound to find the guy of your dreams.

If your Rising Sign is CANCER (♋), you have an intelligent face with twinkling eyes and a smiling mouth. Your hair is very fine and it's often either very blonde or very dark – invariably dyed. Cancer rules the bosom and you certainly have one large enough for all your mates to use as a pillow (metaphorically speaking of course!). When you first meet others, you come across as rather tough, even though underneath you're a right old softie. The Cancer motto is "I feel" and this is something which may surprise your mates. But you are, in fact, deeply sensitive and you're not doing yourself any favours by hiding this. See this quality as an asset, not a handicap, and you'll become instantly more attractive.

If your Rising Sign is LEO (♌), you have thick, wavy hair, which you like to wear back off your face. You have a lovely smiley expression and this makes you very attractive to others. As a Leo Rising female, you may be short, but because you have good posture, your lack of stature usually goes unnoticed. Leo rules the heart and when it comes to others your heart is very big indeed. In fact, you strive to make people – especially boys – like you and would be well miffed if you discovered that someone

– *anyone* – found you disagreeable. The Leo motto is "I create" and so it should be – because you're a very imaginative person. If your life ever gets boring, you'll do whatever you can to liven it up. And if you get totally tired of being you (which seems to happen from time to time), you're perfectly capable of using your creative powers to re-invent yourself. Which is fine as long as the real you doesn't get lost in the process.

If your Rising Sign is VIRGO (♍), you're a lively, chatty person with an inquisitive nature and expression. You're probably tall and, although you may be slim, you're destined to fill out as you get older! However horizontally challenged you become though, you'll always have fab legs! You may feel a bit of a wimp sometimes, but Virgo rules the stomach; maybe that's why other people see you as having plenty of guts! If something displeases you, you're certainly not going to sit there in silence – oh no. If a complaint's being made, it's more than likely Miss Virgo Rising who's making it! The Virgo motto is "I serve", which sounds a bit sad, but just illustrates how willing you are to help others. In a romantic relationship, you do run the risk of being taken for granted, so it's important that you make yourself clear at the very start. You're fussy about boyfriends, but in your view the fewer you date, the fewer you have to dump and the more fun you have.

If your Rising Sign is LIBRA (♎), you're gorgeously female and attractive, with a shapely figure and a pretty face. You're average to tall in height and have beautiful hair. Libra rules the spine and no one who knows you would ever call you spineless. In fact, you have your own particular brand of courage and forthrightness, which occasionally translates as arrogance but is often charming. This doesn't wash with your female friends, but goes down a treat with the blokes, who seem to interpret it as a kind of sexual confidence. The Libra motto is "I consider", which *should* make you discerning but in actual fact means you'll basically consider anyone! You find it very hard to say "no" to boys and this can get you into tricky situations. And although you like an easy life, you don't mind a romantic complication every now and again.

If your Rising Sign is SCORPIO (♏), you have an unusual face, with a well-defined jawline, a wide mouth and amazing eyes. Your figure is curvy (though not necessarily slim) and your hair is thick and naturally wavy. You're an inquisitive person by nature – this

may be heightened by the fact that the sign of Scorpio rules the nose! Other people see you as a real cool customer and a few may even be a bit scared of you. They know how clever and intuitive you are and because you give the impression that you're hard, they may regard you as a force to be reckoned with. Which, of course, you are . . . The Scorpio motto is "I control" and, it has to be said, you are a bit of a control freak, especially when it comes to relationships. You're the original bossy madam and won't take any nonsense from people – blokes especially – who won't do as they're told!

If your Rising Sign is SAGITTARIUS

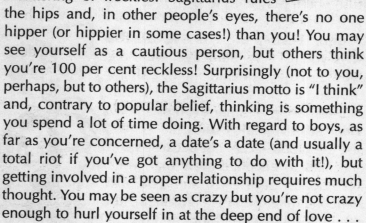

(♐), you're tall and slim, your face is oval, and your expression is open and honest. Your hair is thick and wavy and is either red or very dark. You have bright eyes, arched eyebrows and a smattering of freckles. Sagittarius rules the hips and, in other people's eyes, there's no one hipper (or hippier in some cases!) than you! You may see yourself as a cautious person, but others think you're 100 per cent reckless! Surprisingly (not to you, perhaps, but to others), the Sagittarius motto is "I think" and, contrary to popular belief, thinking is something you spend a lot of time doing. With regard to boys, as far as you're concerned, a date's a date (and usually a total riot if you've got anything to do with it!), but getting involved in a proper relationship requires much thought. You may be seen as crazy but you're not crazy enough to hurl yourself in at the deep end of love . . .

If your Rising Sign is CAPRICORN (♑), you're small and slim with a boyish air. You have thin, straight hair – dark most probably – a long face and a serious demeanour. Capricorn rules the teeth and the skeleton – perhaps that's why other people see you as someone who, once you've got your teeth into something, is like a dog with a bone! And you make no bones about letting other people see the real you either, the only difference between your opinion and theirs being that they see you as a rather sweet person. You're pretty hard on yourself, but that sort of modesty makes others warm to you. The Capricorn motto is "I learn" and that's something you do every minute of the day, especially with regard to relationships. Romantically, you aren't the sort who leaps at the chance of going out with the first bloke who fancies you: in fact, until you *really* have a boy's trust, you'll play hard to get . . .

If your Rising Sign is AQUARIUS (♒), you're very attractive with big eyes, a slightly "Roman" nose, a sharp chin and a sexy smile. You're tall and slim with long legs, narrow hips and a small bust. Aquarius rules the veins and the blood – very apt because no one likes to circulate more than you! You have loads of friends and you can somehow be someone different to each of them. You need different people for different reasons and not all the people you meet and get to know realize this. So people are often surprised when they discover that there's more to you than initially meets the eye. The Aquarian motto is "I adapt" and, it's true, you can be a complete chameleon when you need to be – socially and more so when it comes to relationships. This can confuse some blokes – especially when you jump from one personality to another! – but others (a special few, admittedly) find this a most endearing quality . . .

If your Rising Sign is PISCES (♓), you have huge glittery eyes and a figure to die for. You're easy to spot because, although you always manage to look cool, you're such a scruff: if the hem of your skirt's hanging down or buttons are missing from your shirt, you're definitely a Pisces Rising girl! Pisces rules the feet and it's no secret that you're always opening your mouth and putting your trotter in it! Generally, you're seen as someone who couldn't really care less what others think of her. But that's not entirely true (you wouldn't be reading this if it was, would you?) and your main reason for appearing that way is because you don't want people to think it's up to them to build up your self-esteem. The Piscean motto is "I believe", making you very trusting, gullible even. Many a bloke has won your heart by spouting a load of old romantic codswallop and you, like a true Pisces Rising, have fallen for it. Better luck next time; and there *will* be a next time, don't doubt it for a second . . .

The Pisces + Rising Sign Combinations
The combination of your Sun Sign – Pisces – with your Rising Sign is very important when it comes to your attitude towards the opposite sex.

If your **Rising Sign** is **Aries** and your Sun Sign is Pisces, you are crazy for love and romance, but tend to spread yourself a little too thinly. Give more to one guy and you'll be happier all round.

If your **Rising Sign** is **Taurus** and your Sun Sign is Pisces, you're a one-man woman and proud of it too! Brief flings just aren't your "thing": you'd much rather put all your energy into one romance at a time.

If your **Rising Sign** is **Gemini** and your Sun Sign is Pisces, the thought of a committed relationship repels you. You may change, but in the meantime, a string of brief encounters will do just fine.

If your **Rising Sign** is **Cancer** and your Sun Sign is Pisces, you want total commitment from a guy. And this could be asking a bit much – especially when you only met him last night!

If your **Rising Sign** is **Leo** and your Sun Sign is Pisces, you often end up going out with guys, not because you like them, but because you don't like being without a boyfriend. This is something you should avoid.

If your **Rising Sign** is **Virgo** and your Sun Sign is Pisces, you want a lot from the blokes in your life but rarely get it. Maybe you should be less demanding . . .

If your **Rising Sign** is **Libra** and your Sun Sign is Pisces, you don't feel complete unless you're embroiled in a love affair. That's why you hang on in there, even when it's clear the thrill has gone.

If your **Rising Sign** is **Scorpio** and your Sun Sign is Pisces, you're doubly emotional and seriously possessive. In turn, this can cause the blokes you fancy to run a mile as soon as they see you approach.

If your **Rising Sign** is **Sagittarius** and your Sun Sign is Pisces, your love life is problematic. This is because you allow friends to interfere. Remember, it's you – not your mates – who's going out with the guy.

If your **Rising Sign** is **Capricorn** and your Sun Sign is Pisces, your love life is unpredictable. You believe that romance is controlled by Fate – and not by you at all. And because you allow it to be, it is!

If your **Rising Sign** is **Aquarius** and your Sun Sign is Pisces, you're not in a big rush to get into a long-term relationship and may choose to settle down much later than your friends. Fair enough.

If you're a double Pisces – in that your Sun Sign and **Rising Sign** are **Pisces** – you think nothing of having two or three boyfriends on the go at any one time. Some would call this two-timing: you call it covering your options . . .

The Secret Life Of Pisces

Everyone knows the characteristics of their star sign, but we all have hidden depths. Check out yours . . .

Pisceans are ruled by the mystical and romantic planet Uranus and this gives you a rather dreamy, head-in-the-clouds and girlie image. This is how you *appear* anyway – how you actually *are* is a different matter altogether . . . Hidden beneath that muddled and vague exterior lies a rather together and manipulative person. The confused, little-girl-lost act is just that – an act. If you want something, you'll get it – and make it look as if you came by it purely by chance too! Although you act as if a small gust of wind might blow you away, you're well able to stand up to all the stuff that life throws at you and are able to deal with problems as efficiently as anyone – but only if you have to. If there's someone else around who can – or offers to – do it for you, then it's over to them. Your apparent lack of ambition is an act too – to cover your fear of hard work!

Strengths: Pisceans get a lot of bad press and although they're often described as wishy-washy, they can be remarkably single-minded, strong and determined. You come across as a bit of a hippy, not materialistic in the slightest and without an ounce of ambition, but you – and only you – know that you're not like that at all. You have barrowloads of talent too, but tend to keep this hidden away for fear of being exploited. Not many people know that.

Weaknesses: Your main weakness is that you like others to see you as weak (it can be to your advantage sometimes), but deep down you're pretty tough. You also play on the fact that you're a girl and use this to get your own way with the opposite sex whenever you can. No one can turn on the waterworks like a Piscean! And although you can be optimistic, underneath you're a total defeatist, giving up completely at the first sign of failure.

Fears: The thing that terrifies you most is being without someone to love or of not belonging. You're also frightened of facing up to unpleasant truths (you'd rather ignore them in the hope that they'll go away) and of having to take responsibility for your own actions. (You'd much rather blame someone else!) Other fears include being told what to do, other people knowing too much about you and anything that's grubby and/or unpleasant-looking.

Desires: More than anything, you seek a peaceful and joy-filled existence. You sometimes make out that you don't need romance in your life, but you secretly crave it. You also want all the horrible things in life to vanish. Ideally, you desire a life filled with beautiful music, harmonious relationships, gorgeous little fluffy things and beautiful people. Oh, and although you outwardly don't place much importance on money, you'd secretly like a big pile of cash too.

Secret talent: Because you're so modest, you'd have everyone believe that you were a total talent-free zone. But you're not. One such skill is writing – especially poetry. Another is performing magic tricks. If you've never tried it, it's about time you started learning how it's done!

As a girlfriend . . . although you can be gorgeously romantic and eager to please, you can also be quietly manipulative. You often come across as rather helpless and pathetic to the opposite sex, but this is just a ploy to get the guys to see you as harmless. And although you strike many a potential boyfriend as very laid-back and easy-going, once you've got your claws into him, you're as possessive as hell. Demanding too. In reality, and despite the sweet smile, you're as well able to chew blokes up and spit 'em out as the next man-eater! (Yikes!) You just hide it well, that's all.

As a best friend ... you totally involve yourself in your best chum's life and take her problems as seriously as your own. That's what you'd have people think . . . Deep down, although you love your best buddy to bits, there's no way you'd put her before yourself. And although you're happy to play agony aunt to her, there are times when you'd really rather be doing something a tad more self-indulgent. On the plus side, however, although you like people to believe that you won't stand for any nonsense – not even from your best mate – in reality, you put up with a lot of nonsense. And you don't mind. In fact, mostly you don't even *notice*.

Pisces In Love

Emotional Pisces

Such a romantic soul, you believe whole-heartedly in the power of love. Forever on the lookout for your true soulmate and always able to find a bit of what you want in almost everyone you meet, you can become emotionally confused. Once in a relationship, you're extremely caring, giving your boyfriend all the attention he wants. You'll do absolutely anything for those you love and, as you do it because you enjoy doing it, you don't even need great shows of appreciation in return.

Advice: * Break it to yourself gently that not every cloud has a silver lining. * You don't have to get emotionally involved with every bloke you fancy. * Don't settle for second-best just because you hate being alone. * Don't let your boyfriend walk all over you – because if you let him, he will . . .

Practical Pisces

It's your romantic nature which inspires you to send flowers and fax love notes to your boyfriend or bloke you fancy. And it's your general moodiness which can make you come across as a bit whiney. On the surface you appear gentle – almost helpless at times. OK, so you might not be any good at putting up shelves or changing light bulbs, but when it comes to dealing with the more practical side of love, underneath it all you're no less well equipped than any of the other signs. You do have problems making major decisions though and are always grateful for a helping hand when they need to be made. You can make a bloke believe that you share all his interests and that you'll happily join him when he goes bungee jumping, but once you've got him hooked (quite literally!), you'll manage to wriggle out of it.

Advice: * Don't moan on at your boyfriend just because you're in that sort of mood. * Show him you can look after yourself – he'll respect your independence. * Don't always expect to be bailed out – you won't be. * Don't make up stories to get you out of trouble.

Piscean Love Crises

You've been blessed (some would say cursed) with the ability to delude yourself, and if a relationship is going sour, you find it quite easy to pretend everything's just fine. You just cut yourself off and sink back into your own little fantasy world. This can be infuriating for any bloke you're seeing, who may not be able to get through to you when he most needs to. You can be secretive too and your "not telling you" attitude can drive even the most reasonable boyfriend to distraction. Crises can also occur when your "intended" feels completely swamped by your love – and even you have to admit that you can go a bit "fatal attraction" on a bloke at times. More problems can arise from infidelity. Because you're quite likely to stray yourself (and this is down to a lack of self-control more than anything), if your boyfriend indulges in any extra-curricular activity, you're more likely to turn a blind eye than erupt with rage. His or your infidelity is usually either a cry for attention or an indication that your relationship needs some work, and you ignoring him isn't going to do anything to help improve the situation.

Advice: * Don't hide from the truth. * Bear in mind that it's not funny to taunt and tease your boyfriend (or even the bloke you fancy) with unnecessary secretiveness. * Don't overdo it on the affection front.

In short . . .

They Love You . . . because you're just so incredibly sweet. You're friendly, gentle and caring too, and make almost every boy you meet feel protective towards you. You make yourself popular by always seeing everything from the other person's point of view. And although you seem as soft, daft and helpless as a cuddly toy on the surface, you're deeply philosophical and very strong on the inside.

They Leave You . . . because you can be very jealous

and insecure. You're gullible too and let people take advantage of you. You can be quite hard work because you need constant confidence-boosting and you're completely impractical about everything. Even when you know a relationship isn't happening, you still cling on for dear life and that can be quite off-putting to any potential long-term boyfriends.

When You Fall In Love . . . you're at your happiest. You often delude yourself though by thinking that the boy of your dreams is perfect in every way. When you discover he's not, you may feel let down.

Check this Piscean compatibility chart to discover who you're likely to have a crush on, who you tend to date, who you fall in love with, and who's best kept as a friend. Check the key for ratings.

His Sign	You'd have a CRUSH on . . .	You tend to DATE . . .	You could LOVE . . .	You're just good FRIENDS with . . .
Aries				✿
Taurus			✿	
Gemini	❤		❤	
Cancer		▶	❤	
Leo				▶
Virgo			▶	▶
Libra				▶
Scorpio		✿	✿	▶
Sagittarius				▶
Capricorn				▶
Aquarius	▶		✿	▶
Pisces		✿		

Key: ❤ = In a major way   ✿ = When you're in the mood   ▶ = In a minor way

Which Pisces Are You?

As you already know, being born between February 19 and March 19 makes you a Pisces. But contrary to popular belief, there isn't just one type of Pisces. There are actually four. The one you are depends on your date of birth. Check below and see whether you're Miss Rollercoaster, Miss Special, Miss Passionate or Miss Dreamer . . .

Born February 19–25?
You're MISS ROLLERCOASTER

Born close to the sign of Aquarius, but under the sign of Pisces, you're known as Aquarius-Pisces Cusp. This combination can cause plenty of inner conflict; you have the energy and broad-mindedness of an Aquarian, but the quiet idealism of a Piscean. If you can successfully mix these aspects of your personality together, you're sure to do well in life. But if you allow one side of your character to outweigh or overwhelm the other, you could have problems. More than anything, you want to live life to the full. Trouble is, you're so sensitive that many of the things you force yourself to experience are quite upsetting and/or stressful for you. You need to bear in mind that life doesn't have to be a series of massive highs and lows; and that sometimes it's nice to stay on an even keel, even if you feel you're missing something.

Born February 26—March 4?
You're MISS SPECIAL

You're an extremely spiritual person and have a general dislike for the material world. You love art, music, literature and could well have strong religious beliefs. You hate money and what it's capable of doing to people. You have the ability to see the beauty in everything and tend to go out of your way to find it. You are dedicated, devoted and loyal – and these traits are applied more to your work and personal interests than to your family and friends. This isn't a huge problem, but the way you tend to see yourself as "special" can be. You can also really irritate others by making out you're always right and this can bring about much unwanted friction. Try to remain aware of the needs of the people around you: sometimes you get so wrapped up in your own little world, you forget about the other folk in your life.

Born March 5—11?
You're MISS PASSIONATE

Of all the Piscean types, you're the most intense. You like to spend a lot of time alone and hate being surrounded by loads of people you barely know. You have a small group of friends who can provide you with all the love and support you need. Because of this, you rarely look outside this group. This can make you appear anti-social, but you're not: you just have no desire to acquire more mates than necessary. You're extremely close to your friends – happy to share everything with them. You often feel different and could well have suffered because of this: that's why you appreciate your friends so much. You're very excitable – some would say passionate – and because of a deep longing to feel alive, you hurl yourself in at the deep end of everything, ensuring you have some weird and wonderful (sometimes frightening) experiences.

Born March 12–19?
You're MISS DREAMER

You're the most sensitive and psychic of all the Piscean types and, although you like to think that you'll probably end up using your gifts to help other people in some way, this may not actually happen unless you make a huge effort to do so. The trouble with you is that you can never quite make up your mind what you want from life: you might know what you should do, but actually doing it is another matter altogether. You're so broad-minded (some would call it wishy-washy), you can always see everything from everyone's point of view. In theory, this should be an advantage, but in effect it's disastrous. You have high expectations with regards to what you want, but make no real effort to go about getting it. Then you wonder why you don't get what you want. This is your main quandary. To change things, you need to be more decisive, more definite about your opinions and more active in seeking out your desires.

Part 2:

Looks

It's often easy to identify a person's star sign by their looks and physique. In this chapter you'll find a description of the typical appearance of a Pisces. If this doesn't quite fit, however, it doesn't necessarily mean you're not a typical Pisces – it simply means that other factors, including your Rising Sign (see pages 6–19), have influenced your image. Sometimes, the combination of your Rising Sign and your Sun Sign gives you a more "mixed" look. So don't be alarmed if it doesn't sound like you. You're just that bit more intriguing!

Pisces – The Proud Princess!

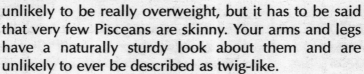

You believe that if you've got it you should flaunt it, but perhaps that's because you've most definitely got it! Pisceans are extremely feminine looking, with ample bosoms (when they grow), a tiny waist, well-rounded hips and bum and a really sexy walk. The typical Piscean body is short in height and curvaceous in build. You're unlikely to be really overweight, but it has to be said that very few Pisceans are skinny. Your arms and legs have a naturally sturdy look about them and are unlikely to ever be described as twig-like.

Top tip: Keep an eye on your posture – the way you slouch can really let you down sometimes.

If you want to find out more about your body – and compare your looks to those of the other eleven signs – check the chart opposite . . . (But remember that some of you won't have the typical looks for your sign.)

Body Beautiful? Check the chart below and find out . . .

Your Sign	Height-wise you're . . .	Build-wise you're . . .	Best feature is your . . .	Worst feature is your . . .	You come across as . . .	You'd be fit if you weren't . . .
PISCES	short	thickset	chest	feet	warm	self-pitying
ARIES	medium/tall	big-boned	shoulders	scar/s(?!)	big and bold	accident prone
TAURUS	medium/tall	sturdy	neck	shoulders	cuddly	lazy
GEMINI	short/medium	slight	arms	skin	small and cute	faddy
CANCER	short/medium	chunky	skin	chest	soft	such a hypochondriac
LEO	short	slim but solid	posture	ankles	tough	arrogant
VIRGO	medium/tall	slender	legs	nails	clean	fussy
LIBRA	medium	curvy	waist	bum	sexy	indecisive
SCORPIO	medium	stocky	bum	legs	strong	self-destructive
SAGITTARIUS	medium/tall	athletic	thighs	hips	very fit	impatient
CAPRICORN	short	small	ankles	knees	earthy	fatalistic
AQUARIUS	tall	strong	hands	calves	unusual	unwilling

Fit For Anything!

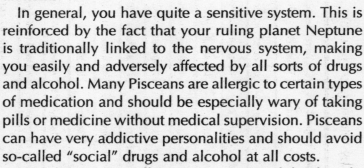

The body area associated with Pisceans is the feet. Blisters, bunions and corns are typically Piscean ailments.

In general, you have quite a sensitive system. This is reinforced by the fact that your ruling planet Neptune is traditionally linked to the nervous system, making you easily and adversely affected by all sorts of drugs and alcohol. Many Pisceans are allergic to certain types of medication and should be especially wary of taking pills or medicine without medical supervision. Pisceans can have very addictive personalities and should avoid so-called "social" drugs and alcohol at all costs.

You're not a naturally sporty person and the thought of participating in team or competitive sports fills you with dread. If you want to keep fit, swimming is a good way of doing it. Yoga, too, can be beneficial and help alleviate stress. Dancing and ice-skating may also appeal to you.

Top Tip: Go barefoot whenever you get the chance: it's good to get some air to those sensitive trotters!

If you want to find out more about your health – and also see how fit the other eleven signs are – check the chart opposite . . .

Find out how to stay on top form by referring to this chart . . .

Your Sign	The most vulnerable part of your body	Most frequent illness	You have accidents . . .	Stay healthy by . . .
PISCES	feet	being generally unwell	because your head's in the clouds	staying alert
ARIES	head	headaches	with sharp things	working out
TAURUS	throat	sore throats	because of your clumsiness	eating healthily
GEMINI	arms and hands	coughs	because you get so stressed out	doing yoga
CANCER	chest	indigestion	because you get so tired	improving your diet
LEO	back	backache	because you are always showing off	expressing yourself
VIRGO	stomach	tummy ache	because you're always so tense	relaxing more
LIBRA	kidneys	urinary infections	because you overdo it	exercising more
SCORPIO	reproductive organs	menstrual problems	with hot things	not ignoring problems
SAGITTARIUS	hips and thighs	feeling run-down	when playing sport	calming down a bit
CAPRICORN	knees	colds	because you work too hard	working less
AQUARIUS	calves and ankles	allergies	with your ankles	slowing down

35

Fashion Victim? Never!

Y ou like to wear soft-textured clothes in unusual styles.

You're not a fashion victim as you like to look different from everyone else. Rummaging around in second-hand markets, in search of all things weird and wonderful, is one of your fave hobbies. As a rule, Pisceans almost always look fab, no matter what they're wearing. On a good day, you can just throw something on and look brilliant: at times like this, you even look cool in your old Minnie Mouse nightshirt! But as a haphazard Piscean, you do have "off" days. The best way to recognize a Piscean is by what they're wearing on their feet. Although you can look smart, your shoes always let you down. If someone's wearing scuffed and/or scruffy shoes, chances are they're a Piscean.

Top Tip: If you really want to make a good impression, you can't just fling on whatever's lying around on your bedroom floor: there *are* times when it's important to really think about what you wear . . .

For more details about what you wear and how you wear it – and to check out how stylish the other eleven signs are – see the chart opposite . . .

More about clothes on the chart below . . .

Your Sign	Your clothes must be . . .	The colour that suits you best is . . .	Your best thing to wear is a . . .	Your fave fabric is . . .	Favourite shop
PISCES	pretty	grey	pair of platforms	velvet	Shelly's
ARIES	a statement	red	fab hat	wool	Accessorize
TAURUS	comfortable	blue	scruffy pair of jeans	denim	Milletts
GEMINI	fashionable	yellow	sexy slip-dress	silk	Knickerbox
CANCER	feminine	sea green	long and girlie dress	lace	Benetton
LEO	noticeable	orange	tiara	lurex	Morgan
VIRGO	clean	white	pair of pinstripe trousers	cotton	Marks & Spencer
LIBRA	flirty	lilac	little A-line skirt	satin	Miss Selfridge
SCORPIO	sexy	black	pair of skintight trousers	leather	French Connection
SAGITTARIUS	sporty	turquoise	wet suit!	rubber	Any sports shop
CAPRICORN	smart	brown	cool skirt suit	linen	Wallis
AQUARIUS	original	bright blue	slinky bikini	lycra	Miss Selfridge

Pretty Pisces

Your face – with its porcelain-smooth skin, big watery eyes, long eye-lashes, well-defined eye-brows, small pouty mouth and cheeky dimples – is quite doll-like, especially when you laugh. Beauty spots are a Piscean trait, so you may have one or more of those. (Supermodel Cindy is a fine example.)

Your hair is fine, soft and silky; it can be worn in long feminine styles, but could be a bit of a pain to look after. Short styles look fab on you and are far more manageable.

Top tip: If you've had your hair a certain way for ages and all your friends and family keep telling you how lovely it is, it may be hard for you to gather up the courage to change it. But if you're sick of it and are keen to go for the chop, do it: you won't regret it!

If you want to find out more about the top end of your body take a peek at the chart opposite and, while you're there, check out the other eleven signs too!

Check out your face and hair on this special chart . . .

Your Sign	Your hair is great because it's . . .	On a bad-hair day it's . . .	Your face shape is . . .	Your eyes are . . .	Your mouth is . . .	Your skin is . . .
PISCES	silky	sparse-looking	babyish	massive!	doll-like	translucent
ARIES	strong	frizzy	square	dark	small	ruddy
TAURUS	soft	a total riot!	rounded	baby-big	pouty	clear
GEMINI	extreme	out of control!	oval	twinkly	always moving!	a pain!
CANCER	gorgeously girlie	messy to the max!	round	small	smiley	soft
LEO	your crowning glory!	a bit OTT	square-jawed	almond-shaped	thin-lipped	dry
VIRGO	squeaky clean!	lank	long	heavy-lidded	narrow	combination
LIBRA	thick	unmanageable	heart-shaped	big and pale	perfect!	smooth
SCORPIO	abundant	floppy	broad	penetrating	sexy	normal
SAGITTARIUS	shiny	flyaway	oblong	wide apart	huge!	freckly
CAPRICORN	heavy	greasy	narrow	sleepy-looking	downturned	oily
AQUARIUS	sleek	fine	wide	sparkly	big	sensitive

Give Yourself A Make-Over!

When it comes to making the most of your facial characteristics, make-up can play a part. In astrology, beauty has a strong connection to the elements – Fire, Earth, Air and Water. Pisces is a Water sign, which means you prefer a sexy, feminine look. Check the characteristics of a Water sign below (you share these with the two other Water signs – Cancer and Scorpio), then give yourself an elementary make-over . . .

As a WATER sign, you:
- Are incredibly romantic
- Are sensitive to the needs, moods and feelings of others
- Need a lot of love, attention and affection
- Can be moody
- Have a fantastic imagination
- Don't mind someone else taking the lead in most situations
- Like art and literature
- Can be talked into doing things you'd rather not do at all
- Are a bit secretive

Go for eye make-up in various shades of sea – it'll really bring out the colour of your irises. Emphasize your lips with pale lip colours and give your face some extra shape with clever application of blushers, shaders and highlighters. Don't bother with foundation – you really don't need it. A light dusting of translucent powder will do just fine – even for a night out on the town. Pay special attention to your hair, especially if you wear it in a long feminine style. Short cuts look best on you, more so if your hair is fine.

Top tip: Don't use too much mascara – one coat'll do: your lashes are long and noticeable enough as they are.

Part 3:

Boy Stuff

Quiz: Who's Your Star Guy?

A lot has been said on the subject of cosmic compatibility, but you may have found that, although you're supposed to be attracted to a particular sign, you just keep going for the "wrong" ones.

This isn't because you're a glutton for punishment – in fact, you may even discover that you get on quite well with these so-called incompatible signs – but is the result of how all the planets were positioned in the heavens at the time of your birth. Although you're a Piscean, there might have been more planets present in another sign – say, Gemini, for example – on the day you were born, causing you to take on more of the characteristics of that sign, and making you more attracted to Air and Fire signs than a typical Piscean would be. It takes an experienced astrologer to work out an individual's birth chart (and nearly everyone's chart is different), but doing this quiz is a simple way of working out which sign is most compatible with **you**, as opposed to your sign. Try it and see . . .

1. Four different boys have the serious hots for you. They're all quite different in appearance. On looks alone, which one would you choose to go out with?

a) Serious expression, medium height with a compact physique
b) Bright-eyed, slim with a cute grin
c) Muscly bod with long limbs, amazing eyes and sexy lips
d) Athletic and masculine-looking with striking facial features and fab hair

2. At a party, you've made it clear that you fancy the guy who's standing alone on the other side of the room. Which course of action would you like him to take?
a) Ask you to dance
b) Smile encouragingly but wait for you to make the first move
c) Show his intentions through body language and meaningful stares
d) Act as cool as he can, to make it a bit more challenging for you

3. You finally get chatting. After a while, it becomes clear that he's more than keen. What happens next?
a) You ask him back to your place
b) He suggests going on somewhere else
c) He snogs you suddenly and passionately
d) Nothing – you're both too shy

4. What sort of clothes would you prefer a bloke to wear on your first date?
a) Anything that suits him
b) Anything fashionable
c) Something sporty or casual but cool-looking

d) A shirt, jacket and trousers in natural fabrics or a smart suit

5. He's taking you out for a meal. Where?

a) Pizza Express

b) McDonald's

c) At a riverside café

d) An "as much as you can eat" carvery

6. As a date, he's . . .

a) Intense, serious and a little bit shy

b) Great – he really knows how to do and say all the right things, but seems to expect a lot in return

c) Talkative, unpredictable, a great laugh

d) A great listener, romantic, giving and considerate

7. Where would you like to go on your second date?

a) Round to his place to eat a takeaway and watch TV

b) To a party or wild nightclub

c) To the cinema or theatre

d) For a picnic in the country

8. What's your attitude towards marriage?

a) It's silly, outmoded and impractical – you can't ever imagine wanting to be married

b) It stops you being yourself – and until you're convinced otherwise you're happy to stay single

c) It's lovely – romantic and secure – you can't wait to walk up that aisle

d) It's a good idea for two people who really love each other to make a commitment – when you meet the right person, you'll definitely tie the knot

9. What, to you, would be the perfect holiday?

a) A real action holiday – pony-trekking, mountaineering or something like that

b) As long as there's a reasonable amount of luxury and you can spend time relaxing, you don't care where you go

c) Anywhere you can sample a bit of culture, unusual food and drink and feel all the more enlightened for it

d) Somewhere that stimulates your imagination and leaves you feeling mentally refreshed

10. Which colour is your favourite?

a) Bright yellow, violet or electric blue

b) Bright red, orange, gold or turquoise

c) Pale blue, pink, any shade of green, navy, brown or white

d) Grey, pale blue, silver, dark red, black or sea green

Now work out your scores, making a note of how many F's, E's, A's and W's you get . . .

1. a – E; b – A; c – W; d – F
2. a – F; b – E; c – W; d – A
3. a – W; b – A; c – F; d – E
4. a – W; b – A; c – F; d – E
5. a – A; b – F; c – W; d – E
6. a – E; b – F; c – A; d – W
7. a – E; b – F; c – A; d – W
8. a – A; b – F; c – W; d – E
9. a – F; b – E; c – A; d – W
10. a – A; b – F; c – E; d – W

If you **scored mostly F,** go to the FIRE section.
If you **scored mostly E,** go to the EARTH section.
If you **scored mostly A,** go to the AIR section.
If you **scored mostly W,** go to the WATER section.

(In the event of a "tie" – i.e., you score equally on two or more sections – you can go to both or all sections indicated and be ultimately equally attracted to two or more different star signs.)

Fire

Fire sign guys are:
* Energetic
* Warm
* Fun-loving
* Passionate
* Enthusiastic
* A little bit crazy

Sound like your type? Now answer this simple question:

Which of the following statements do you most agree with?

a) When I go on a date, I like a guy to be spontaneous and passionate. If he wants more than a goodnight peck on the cheek that's just fine by me.
b) When I go out with a guy, I like to be treated with a substantial amount of respect. I like to have fun, but I hate being rushed and like to take relationships one step at a time.
c) All I want from a boyfriend is a good time. If he's

happy, I'm happy. I've no intentions of getting heavy with a guy – that's the best way to send him running.

*If you answered a) the guy for you is an **Aries**. To find out more about him, turn to page 51.*

*If you answered b) the guy for you is a **Leo**. To find out more about him, turn to page 62.*

*If you answered c) the guy for you is a **Sagittarius**. To find out more about him, turn to page 72.*

Earth

Earth sign guys are:

* Hard-working
* Faithful
* Practical
* Loyal
* Down-to-earth
* A little bit sensible

Sound like your type? Now answer this simple question:

Which of the following qualities do you believe to be the most important in a boyfriend?

a) Serious sexiness

b) A fab sense of humour

c) Immense cleverness

*If you answered a) the guy for you is a **Taurus**. To find out more about him, turn to page 54.*

*If you answered b) the guy for you is a **Virgo**. To find out more about him, turn to page 64.*

*If you answered c) the guy for you is a **Capricorn**. To find out more about him, turn to page 75.*

Air

Air sign guys are:
* Talkative
* Sociable
* Changeable
* Unpredictable
* Interesting
* A little bit "bonkers"

Sound like your type? Now answer this simple question:

Which of the following dates would you prefer?

a) Going to a posh restaurant for dinner, then to see your fave band, then to the best nightclub in town to rave until the early hours.

b) Spending a day in the country, having a snog in a cornfield, followed by supper at an Olde Worlde Inne and a romantic train ride home, watching the sunset through the dusk.

c) Having a champagne breakfast (OK, so you may be under eighteen, but this is fantasy-land here) in a hot air balloon, a nice walk by the river, then on to see a fascinating film at your local cinema.

*If you answered a) the guy for you is a **Gemini**. To find out more about him, turn to page 56.*

*If you answered b) the guy for you is a **Libra**. To find out more about him, turn to page 67.*

*If you answered c) the guy for you is an **Aquarius**. To find out more about him, turn to page 78.*

Water

Water sign guys are:

* Sensitive
* Sentimental
* Mysterious
* Secretive
* Intense
* A little bit weird

Sound like your type? Now answer this simple question:

Which of the following holidays would you like best?

a) A relaxing holiday by the sea, somewhere peaceful, picturesque and romantic.

b) A luxurious holiday in a historical setting, where there are lots of old ruins and places to explore.

c) A sailing holiday in a faraway, beautiful, uncrowded and exotic place.

*If you answered a) the guy for you is a **Cancer**. To find out more about him, turn to page 59.*

*If you answered b) the guy for you is a **Scorpio**. To find out more about him, turn to page 70.*

*If you answered c) the guy for you is a **Pisces**. To find out more about him, turn to page 80.*

Astro-Boys

So you've found your ideal romantic partner . . .
Well, now's the time to check him out good and
proper.

Aries (March 20–April 19)

He's a hero . . . because he's
really popular and has a zillion
mates you can flirt with. Also . . .
* He's honest and straightforward
* He's very affectionate
* He's sexy to the max
* He loves to spring little surprises
  on you
* Everyone thinks he's fab
* He's a top snogger!!

He's a zero . . . when he acts creepy
around girls (he could smarm for
Britain!) and two-times (sometimes
three-times) girlfriends. Plus . . .
* He's just too bossy
* He's always ogling other girls
* He tells the occasional "white" lie
* He's a bit of a stirrer
* He won't wait for anyone or anything
* He'll never love you more than he loves himself

Personality Alert!

No matter how much he likes you, you'll never be his number one priority. Because his number one priority is (as if you haven't guessed) . . . himself!

He looks great . . . because he's got a fab body – not an ounce of fat! – a chiselled, model-like face and a sexy expression. He's slim and muscular with wide shoulders and snakey hips. Arien males usually have thick, dark, well-styled hair which they're always touching. Facially, they look much like the animal that represents their sign – a ram! – especially in profile, with a long straight nose, chiselled cheekbones, beetly eyebrows and small mouth and chin. He likes fashionable clothes in bright colours and although he generally favours the sporty look, he will dress up smart if the occasion requires it.

He's a state . . . because he's a bit of a poseur and tends to overdo it with the "designer" labels. (Also, if you don't like the facial characteristics of a ram, then he may not be your cup of tea . . .)

Meet him . . .
– wherever there's a football.
– getting on down at the grooviest club in town.
– in McDonald's – on either side of the counter.

Impress him by . . . being totally upfront. If you fancy him, don't be shy: tell him. He'll love you for it! To catch his attention, wear something bright (in his team's colours preferably). If he compliments you, be grateful, but don't let him see you flirt with other guys – that's something he can't stand.

If you can't be bothered to do the running . . . then that won't be a problem. He loves the thrill of the chase, so once he gets wind of you fancying him, he'll be straight in there! He certainly doesn't beat around the metaphorical bush when it comes to chatting up girls, so chances are he'll just come and tell you if he fancies you (unfortunately, he'll also tell you just as loud and clear if he doesn't!) He's a great snogger – and he knows it – so he may just lunge for your lips before he's even spoken to you! Scary or what?!

Keep him by . . . never bossing him around (especially in front of his mates); being mega-appreciative when he's nice to you; telling him you love him at every opportunity; not flirting with other blokes; showing him what a totally cool and busy chick you are!

Dump him when . . . you find him snogging your best mate. (And you will.)

Love match: If you're a Leo, a Libran or a Sagittarian, you're putty in his hands!

Top Arien totty: Mark Hamilton (Ash), Damon Albarn, Linford Christie, Coree (Damage), Will Mellor, Robert Downey Jnr and Paul Nicholls.

Taurus (April 20–May 20)

He's a hero . . . because of his loving, gentle nature. He's loyal to those he loves and, whether you're his mate or his girlfriend, he'll stand by you at all times. Also . . .

* He has masses of sex appeal (and doesn't even know it!)
* He'll listen to your problems all day and all night
* He's modest, kind and reliable
* He makes you go all quivery whenever he touches you
* He's very romantic

He's a zero . . . because he's the King Of Self-Indulgence and barely notices you exist sometimes! Plus . . .

* He's a bit of a couch potato
* His temper can get out of control
* He can't always keep up with you
* His moods are too much to take sometimes
* He can be self-obsessed
* He's hideously stubborn

Personality Alert!

His worst nightmare comes true when you finally discover that, underneath it all, he is in fact very boring! Oh no!!

He looks great . . . because he's super-cuddly and mega-cute. And he's got a million woolly jumpers that he won't mind lending you (only when you're his girlfriend of course . . .). He has a clear complexion, a sweet little mouth and gorgeous eyes. Most Taurus guys love clothes – and while they like the idea of looking trendy, they tend to dress down, preferring comfortable clothes in natural colours and fabrics. Show him a little something in Lycra and he'll run a mile!

He's a state . . . mainly because sometimes he just can't be bothered and, looks-wise, could give Swampy a run for his money! Also, he's a right old sloucher – it's sometimes hard to tell the difference between a Taurean bloke on a sofa and a sack of spuds!

Meet him . . .
- round at his place (he doesn't get out much!)
- round his mate's house (he rarely has more than one close male friend).
- in the local greasy caff (he really enjoys a good fry-up!)

Impress him by . . . enjoying lazing around as much as he does and taking the lead when it comes to getting physical. He's very tactile, so when you're there on the sofa with him, touch him at every opportunity. He likes girls who are relaxed and know how to have a good time. He's a bit worried about being boring and stupid though, so don't tease him in any way – especially in front of his mates. (Or should we say mate?!)

If you can't be bothered to do the running . . . you could have a problem. He's a shy guy at the best of times, so don't expect him to bowl you over with his bird-pulling tactics. If he so much as smiles at you across a crowded room, he thinks he's being pushy. He takes his time working out who he fancies, but once he's made up his mind, he'll make sure he's near you at all times, giving you the chance to make *your* move on *him*. Very subtle . . .

Keep him by . . . having a fab sense of humour; being open about your feelings; not taking the mickey out of him; not snogging or fighting him in public; giving him the time and space he needs, especially when it comes to making decisions.

Dump him when . . . he asks for his jumpers back.

Love match: If you're a Virgo, Scorpio or Capricorn, you're the girl for him.

Top Taurean totty: Jas Mann (Babylon Zoo), Jay Darlington (Kula Shaker), Harry Enfield, Lance (N-Sync), Emilio Estevez and Sean Conlon (5ive) .

Gemini (May 21–June 20)
He's a hero . . . because he's a social chameleon and you can take him anywhere! He has opinions on every subject and loves a chat. He's also broad-minded, but PC at the same time. Also . . .

* He gets on with all your mates
* He's a real good laugh
* He's ever so romantic
* Life's never dull when he's around
* He's a big kid

He's a zero . . . because, as he's so easily bored, he can make you feel boring! He's moody to the max and can be horribly irritable. He also "forgets" dates and can be immature. Plus . . .

* He's too demanding
* He's totally unpredictable
* He won't stop flirting
* He thinks nothing of dating two (or even three) girls at a time
* He's a huge show-off

Personality Alert!

He may look like butter wouldn't melt in his mouth, but he's the best liar in the zodiac. So be prepared to be foiled!

He looks great . . . because his tall, slim physique makes him look quite model-like. He has a sweet face, with twinkly eyes and a very naughty expression.

He's a state . . . because his sense of "style" (if you can call it that) leaves a lot to be desired. He loves to be trendy, but gets it totally wrong sometimes and ends up looking like a rather sad fashion victim. And what's with all the daft hats?! If any bloke makes you feel like calling the Fashion Police, it'll be Mr Gemini!

Meet him . . .
- at the trendiest hot spot in town.
- on a bus, train or plane.
- in a mobile phone showroom.

Impress him by . . . telling him you fancy him in five different languages (he likes clever – and straight-talking – chicks!) or asking him to help you with *The Times* crossword. And when you get chatting to him, make sure you laugh at all his jokes (even the totally surreal ones!) Once you've located him, you must play it as cool as he does. Never show your jealous side (if you've got one) and try to maintain an air of mystery.

If you can't be bothered to do the running . . . don't expect him to come running after you. This guy never makes much effort when it comes to pulling – mainly because he doesn't have to. His looks mean that you can't fail to notice him, but if he fancies you, he will use his ability to bewitch you from a distance, without saying a word. A Gemini boy can make you feel "drawn" to him and, no matter how shy you are, you'll suddenly find that you're the one doing all the work! Note: once in his clutches it may be hard to escape!

Keep him by . . . being very understanding (telepathic preferably!); staying faithful (even when he's not!);

putting up with his moods; spending most of your time together talking about him.

Dump him when . . . he stops returning your phone calls, and starts making up crap excuses about where he's been and what he's been doing.

Love match: He can only have a long-term relationship with Libran, Sagittarian or Aquarian girls.

Top Geminian totty: Lenny Kravitz, Johnny Depp, Noel Gallagher and Jason Brown (5ive).

Cancer (June 21–July 22)

He's a hero . . . because, most of the time, he's kind, caring, sensitive and trustworthy. He also cooks a mean roast dinner! Also . . .

* He's mega-romantic
* He'll never let you down
* He really understands you
* He'll love you more than anyone has ever loved you
* He's honest and sincere
* He won't hear a bad word said against you

He's a zero . . . because he's mega-crabby, secretly compares his girlfriends to his mum (and it's unlikely

any of them will live up to *her* angelic image), and can be unbelievably selfish. Plus . . .
* He spoils all your fun
* He winds you up like nobody else
* He's a bit of a drama queen!
* He thinks he's always in the right
* He wants everyone to feel sorry for him all the time

Personality Alert!

He can be clingier than cling film and twice as suffocating! Shaking him off could prove difficult.

He looks great . . . with his high cheekbones and charming smile. His clothes are generally pretty cool, and so they should be: they cost enough! He has a rather distinctive face with well-defined features and a friendly expression.

He's a state . . . when he takes the "baggy" look too far and the crotch of his jeans is hovering way below knee level! And, although he's probably slim, he's able to pile on the pounds easily – and, sometimes when he gets involved in a relationship, he lets himself go and gets to be a right old bloater!

Meet him . . .
– beside the seaside (or anywhere there's water really).
– in an amusement arcade (he loves computer games).
– at home, eating a slap-up tea.

Impress him by . . . telling him loads of intimate stuff about yourself and avoiding asking him any nosy questions about himself. Also, as Cancer boys love a snack, share your Rolos with him and he'll be yours for life!

If you can't be bothered to do the running . . . it could take some time before he'll chase you. He's a bit shy so he's not going to make the first move, no matter how many hints you give him. If he even vaguely suspects that you don't like him he'll run a mile. If you make the first move, he'll respond quickly and usually positively. Most Cancer guys, once they're sure of your feelings, can get very romantic and will try to woo you in all the traditional ways – with flowers, poetry, love letters . . . the works!

Keep him by . . . telling him you'll love him forever; being a total tower of strength; standing up for him even when you think he's in the wrong; always taking his opinions and his ideas seriously; being faithful; making him believe he can trust you.

Dump him when . . . he stops and gazes wistfully in the window of Ratners every time you go shopping!

Love match: When he settles, it'll be with a Scorpian, Capricornian or Piscean chick.

Top Cancerian totty: Jamie Redknapp, George Michael, Keith Duffy and Shane Lynch (Boyzone), Tom Cruise, Terry Caldwell (East 17), Prince William and Ross Kemp (EastEnders).

Leo (July 23–August 22)

He's a hero . . . because he's manly, sexy and in control. He's also very generous and great fun to go out with. Also . . .

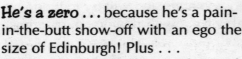

* He loves a good cuddle
* He buys you tons of pressies
* He's majorly optimistic
* He'll take good care of you
* He'll always forgive you

He's a zero . . . because he's a pain-in-the-butt show-off with an ego the size of Edinburgh! Plus . . .

* He's always telling you what to do
* He needs constant flattery
* He fancies himself more than he fancies you
* He's too demanding
* He expects you to drop all your mates in favour of him

Personality Alert!

He can be totally embarrassing – especially when he insists on giving you massive snogs in public!

He looks great . . . as he's a fine figure of a lad with broad shoulders and lush hair. He may not be that lofty, but his posture is good and he strides around in a very "tall" and purposeful way. His face is unusual and usually has something feline about it – slightly slanty eyes perhaps . . . or whiskers maybe! (A lot of post-adolescent Leo guys favour a goatee beard!)

He's a state . . . because he wears too much jewellery (how many chains can a guy drape round one neck?), his hair is too coiffeured (à la The Bee Gees circa 1976), and his "look" is just a bit too considered (i.e. you can tell he spends hours in front of the mirror).

Meet him . . .
– at a gig (one where his band is playing).
– at the theatre (he'll be the star of the show).
– at the cash-point machine (he always has a good wad on him!).

Impress him by . . . flattering him all the time (it'll get you everywhere!) and by being totally committed, dependent even (he likes a girl who brings out the chauvinist in him!). Flattery gets you absolutely everywhere with this guy – no line is too corny! Compliment him on his clothes, his hair, his bike – anything! – and he'll be instantly smitten. He likes lively, upfront girls, so skulking around waiting for him to make the first move won't impress him. Oh – and if you want to make him yours, you should be supermodel gorgeous (although preferably slightly lower on the beauty scale than himself – he hates to be outshone!).

If you can't be bothered to do the running . . . he's sure as hell too proud to make a move on you. He's so wrapped up in himself, he won't have time to waste chasing girls. If he fancies you, he'll let you know in quite an obvious way but will then sit back and expect you to do all the running. His ego won't allow him to do it any other way!

Keep him by . . . being naturally beautiful (he doesn't ask for much, this guy); always paying your way (he's generous but hates being taken for granted); never criticizing him; being ready to party at the drop of a hat.

Dump him when . . . he starts telling you that, more than anything, you've always been a really good friend to him.

Love match: He'll find long-term love with a Sagittarian, Aquarian or Arien female.

Top Leo totty: Matt Le Blanc, Sean Moore (Manic Street Preachers), Arnie Schwarzenegger, Fatboy Slim, David Duchovny and Christian Slater.

Virgo (August 23–September 22)

He's a hero . . . with a brilliant sense of humour – he's the wittiest sign of the zodiac – and a helpful, sympathetic and protective nature. Highly desirable. Also . . .

* He's very clever
* He's extremely cool
* He's never late
* He likes a laugh
* He's fussy about who he goes out with – if he's chosen you, you *must* be special!

He's a zero . . . because his analytical and critical nature can be off-putting. He can also be a bit grumpy and over-demanding. Plus . . .

* He's always putting you down
* He makes a right song and dance about everything you do
* He's a bit mean
* He thinks you're lucky to be in any way connected to him
* He rarely says anything nice to you
* He's emotionally repressed

Personality Alert!

He can pick so many holes in you that you could feel like a colander by the end of your first date!

He looks great . . . with his bright eyes, faintly "amused" expression and spotlessly clean and immaculately ironed clothes. Virgo blokes are attractive – in their own quirky little way. Some look a bit delicate – all knees, elbows and knobbly bits! Most have narrow faces, bright eyes, long noses, thin lips, pointy chins and fine hair. He wears clean, well-pressed clothes in natural fabrics (such as cotton, wool and silk) – classy!

He's a state . . . only first thing in the morning. And even then, his 'jamas are only a teensy bit crumpled! His only other fashion crime is that he does seem to favour narrow-legged trousers and will insist on donning his "drainpipes" even when everyone else is flaunting their flares.

Meet him . . .
- in the supermarket (he's the one referring to a really long list).
- in the chemist's or health food shop (he's always got something wrong with him and in need of cures).
- in the hairdresser's (he has his hair trimmed at least twice a month!)

Impress him by . . . being a "quality bird" (he hates cheapness of any description) and not being coarse or over the top when attempting to pull him. Once you get chatting, don't laugh when he harps on about all his ailments (and he has lots); try to stay chirpy (if there's any moaning to be done, *he* wants to be the one doing it!); and make a point of being very (*very*) interested in everything he says.

If you can't be bothered to do the running . . . don't worry – as long as he's confident you like him, he'll have no qualms about making a move on you. If a Virgo bloke is trying to pull you, you may not notice at first – he's *that* subtle (some would say devious!) When chatting you up, he'll try all his best one-liners on you and have you in fits of laughter. Once he's got you hooked though, he gets really serious and, to some girls, this can be impressive in itself.

Keep him by . . . being 100 per cent devoted; allowing him to impress other girls with his witty quips (he's not flirting – honest!); never gossiping about him with your mates; being mega-sensitive when it comes to his feelings; not springing surprises on him.

Dump him when . . . you start to feel like one of his many ailments.

Love match: If he wants to meet his match, he should be looking for a Capricorn, Pisces or Taurus.

Top Virgoan totty: Keanu Reeves, Charlie Sheen, Hugh Grant, Paul Winterhart (Kula Shaker), Jarvis Cocker, Liam Gallagher and Jimmy Constable (911).

Libra (September 23– October 22)

He's a hero . . . because he has very strong beliefs and is a great mediator. When you come over all "damsel in distress", he's the guy to save you.

Also . . .

* He's sensitive, sensual and sexy
* He'll tell you all the things you want to hear
* He's a great listener
* He's very polite
* He's great to go out with
* His moods are pretty constant
* He's pretty smart

He's a zero . . . because he's vain, superficial, manipulative and so charming he makes you feel sick sometimes. Plus . . .

* He flirts too much
* He's lazy

* He talks a right load of rubbish at times
* He's horribly indecisive
* He's *sooo* impractical
* He's a bit of a fibber

Personality Alert!

He's a sneaky, smarmy snake-in-the-grass, who'll two-time you at the first opportunity. (Oh dear. And he seemed like such a nice chap . . .)

He looks great . . . because he's got dimples, a cheeky smile and a lovely pouty mouth. He looks after his clothes well – even his oldest trackie pants look brand new. His body is athletic-looking, his posture is good and his movements are graceful. He dresses to suit the occasion and can go from looking smart to scruffy, from frumpy to fashionable in a matter of hours. *Fact:* you can spot a Libran bloke by his shoes – he almost always wears baseball boots or trainers.

He's a state . . . because he's got such bad colour coordination, you'd need sunglasses to look at some of his "ensembles". And what's with the baseball cap – is it welded to his head or what?

Meet him . . .
– on a computer course.
– at an after-school/work discussion group.
– in the pet shop (he adores animals!)

Impress him by . . . telling him you're on intimate terms with Robbie Williams and most of All Saints (he loves a lig!), then inviting him to a celebrity bash. (It's not your fault if they all fail to turn up!) If you're interested in this bloke, then above all else you must be easy-going and intelligent. If you're daft or demanding, he won't want to know. He likes a girl to be independent so impress him by parpling on about your numerous extra-curricular activities and your bulging-at-the-seams social diary. To clinch the deal, compliment his looks and comment on his great wit and insight. He's a sucker for flattery!

If you can't be bothered to do the running . . . you won't have to wait long for him to come after you. He'll use his charm, good looks and generosity to attract your attention. He's an expert chatter-upper, so half the time you won't even know he's on the pull. He'll flatter you, be truly fascinated by everything you say and laugh his noggin off at all your jokes.

Keep him by . . . being caring and supportive; allowing him space for his own "interests" (this may or may not include dating other girls. Yikes!); having friends and hobbies of your own; being funny; paying him lots of compliments and springing lavish surprises on him.

Dump him when . . . the flowers he sends you start smelling of guilt.

Love match: He needs a girl who understands him – an Aquarian, Arien or Geminian perhaps.

Top Libran totty: Declan Donnelly, Brett Anderson (Suede), Will Smith and Zac (Zachary Walker) Hanson from Hanson.

Scorpio (October 23–November 22)

He's a hero . . . because he's dynamic, caring and totally unshockable. And, although he's a perfectionist, he's remarkably understanding when it comes to other people's shortcomings. Also . . .

* He's quick-witted and clever
* He can give you everything you need
* He'll really look after you
* He makes you believe he knows you better than you know yourself
* He's got a sexy and mysterious aura
* He can help you get whatever you want

He's a zero . . . because his overwhelming need to be in control can be scary. He's also capable of being hideously self-destructive if things don't go his way. Plus . . .

* He's capable of being dangerously possessive
* He's at the mercy of that green-eyed monster
* He wants to know everything about you but tells you very little about himself
* He thinks he's never wrong
* He makes out he's a real one-woman guy, but he can be unfaithful on a whim

Personality Alert!

He's such a control freak, he'll have you on a dog lead

and signed up for Crufts as soon as you can say "Yes, master (woof!)".

He looks great . . . thanks to those deeply gorgeous eyes and that intense stare. A Scorpio bloke can take on many outward appearances but he's usually casual-but-smartly dressed, well built (though not always tall), with broad shoulders and chest, little snakey hips and a cute butt! He's likely to have a wide forehead, a thick neck, bushy eyebrows and hairy arms(!) All very nice (if you like that kind of thing . . .).

He's a state . . . because sometimes he goes too far with the old macho image and ends up looking like a lumberjack! Plus . . . *Fact:* if a guy has bow-legs, chances are he's a Scorpio!

Meet him . . .
– on the rugby pitch (he loves a scrum or two!)
– in the bookshop, looking for a good thriller or detective novel.
– in bed, watching *Inspector Morse* videos.

Impress him by . . . finding out everything about him before you actually speak to him, then pretending you're psychic! This guy is pretty tricky to ensnare because he has extremely high expectations. He likes to do his own thing so won't necessarily be attracted to you simply because *you* like playing pool too. And anyway, he'd rather you were there in a cheerleader role than in a directly competitive one. If you can prove you're discreet, uncritical and not in the tiniest bit jealous, he *may* just give you a second glance.

If you can't be bothered to do the running . . . that's not a problem – for a short while anyway. If he hears you have the hots for him, he'll be secretly flattered but won't be that obvious in his quest to pull you. His favourite pulling technique is staring. Then he'll take off his shades and stare some more. If that doesn't have the desired effect (i.e. you slavering over him in a matter of minutes), he'll forget all about you and move on to someone who's more receptive to his magnetism.

Keep him by . . . being faithful; being realistic rather than romantic; telling him you're the luckiest girl in the world (why? Because you're going out with him of course!); and never accusing him of being in the wrong (even when he is).

Dump him when . . . he starts blaming you for his self-destructive behaviour.

Love match: The only girls he's truly happy with are Pisceans, Taureans and Cancerians.

Top Scorpian totty: Alonza Bevan (Kula Shaker), Ethan Hawke, Leonardo DiCaprio, Ike (Clarke Isaac) Hanson from Hanson and Alex James (Blur).

Sagittarius (November 23– December 21)

He's a hero . . . because he's honest and fair-minded, always sees the best in people and would never bear a grudge against anyone. He's also a genuinely interesting person and is excellent company. Also . . .

* He can always cheer you up
* He's never boring
* He's always got a smile on his face
* He's your best friend
* Nothing's dull when he's around

He's a zero . . . because he's impatient, reckless and argumentative. And he's always telling people how to run their lives when it's *his* life – more than anyone's – that needs sorting. Plus . . .

* He always seems to be putting his foot in it
* He's really immature
* You can't rely on him
* He can't sit still for a minute
* He's got a bit of an unpredictable temper
* He's incapable of being faithful

Personality Alert!

He's about as easy to lean on as a cloud!

He looks great . . . but only by accident! When you meet him, the first thing you'll notice is his gorgeous legs and bum. If you can drag your eyes upwards, you may notice his big mouth, sparkling eyes and cute little hair "do".

He's a state . . . most of the time. In fact, even on a good day, he looks as if he's covered his body in glue and run backwards through his wardrobe! He's got absolutely no dress sense and anything he wears is usually mismatched, crumpled or just plain grubby. What a scruff!

Meet him . . .
– dreamily reading the special offer cards in travel agents' windows.
– on holiday.
– at a wild party.

Impress him by . . . doing something pretty spectacular – it's the only way you'll ever get him away from the other girls. He likes girls who are as free and easy as he is, so if you're ready to do crazy, impulsive things at a moment's notice, you may be the girl for him. He's not keen on girls who are too grown-up, so coming on all sophisticated with him just won't work.

If you can't be bothered to do the running . . . he's more than happy to do it. He desperately needs to be liked and he'll do anything – including lie – to impress you. He'll try to be cool, but he's not. But his most successful tactic is playing the bumbling idiot – it works a treat every time and may even work on you!

Keep him by . . . telling him you're perfectly happy about having an "open" relationship; constantly reminding him that you've "never felt like this about anyone before" while at the same time not putting any restraints on him (tricky, eh?); inviting him on all your girls' nights out (he won't go but he'll appreciate being asked).

Dump him when . . . he says he's going away for the weekend, then disappears for three months.

Love match: If you're an Arien, Geminian or Leo you'll find this guy totally irresistible.

Top Sagittarian totty: Michael Owen, Ryan Giggs, Gary Lineker, Brad Pitt, Neil Codling (Suede) and Jamie Theakston.

Capricorn (December 22–January 20)

He's a hero . . . because he's brave, realistic and is a great person to turn to for advice. Also, if you're feeling low, he's just the guy to give your ego a boost. Also . . .
* He's loyal
* He always lets you win arguments
* He'll never forget your birthday (or your mum's come to that!)
* You can talk to him about practically anything

He's a zero . . . because he's narrow-minded and refuses to see things from other people's points of view. And, although painfully modest on the surface, deep down he's a tad full of himself. Plus . . .
* He has an overdeveloped dark side (oo-er!)
* He tends to take things the wrong way

* He can be a bit predictable
* He's very insecure
* He won't take any risks
* He's a bit tight with his cash

Personality Alert!

He could drive you mad with his incessant talk of computers!

He looks great ... in his good-quality, expensive gear. He wears a lot of his fave colour – black. But he looks best when his girlfriend dresses him. Because he's a tad conservative, he doesn't particularly stand out, but once you're pointed in his direction, you'll realize how attractive he can be with his bright, intelligent-looking eyes and pixie-ish face.

He's a state ... because he can't do a thing with his hair! It's stuck to his head like seaweed to a rock! It's unlikely that you'll be overwhelmed by this guy's looks, because although he's *kind* of cute, he's not what you'd call a "stunner". And why does he look so *worried* all the time?

Meet him ...
– at the railway station (he's a closet trainspotter!).
– buying CDs (he's a tune-aholic – although he's more Bach than Backstreet!).
– in the library, studying for a "project" (he's such a swot!).

Impress him by ... asking him how fax machines

work or asking him out by e-mail. (He loves girls with an interest in technology.) He likes quiet, sophisticated girls and won't be impressed by anyone loud, crude or raucous. So you can forget about telling him your fave dirty jokes! He likes you to be interested in his hobbies and won't take too kindly to any teasing.

If you can't be bothered to do the running . . . he's not a natural flirt so won't go out of his way to go after you. Most Capricorn guys favour the subtle approach and would rather get a mutual mate to introduce you than approach you. Once he's got your attention, he'll try to blind you with his vast intellect. If you're the type of girl who prefers brain to brawn, this just might work.

Keep him by . . . not yawning when he's talking technology; getting engaged on your first date (he likes to feel secure in a relationship); giving him privacy when he needs it; being quiet and refined; not moaning about his hobbies, even if he spends more time on them than he does on you.

Dump him when . . . you discover his little black book contains more than just the numbers of trains . . .

Love match: If you're a Taurean, a Virgoan or a Cancerian, get on in there!

Top Capricornian totty: Denzel Washington, Tim (Ash), Jim Carrey and Gary Barlow.

Aquarius (January 21– February 18)

He's a hero . . . because he's loyal and deep-thinking. He finds people fascinating and is incredibly observant. If you've got any questions about human behaviour, he's the guy to ask! Also . . .
* He's amusing
* He never seems to get tired
* Everyone likes him
* He'd never two-time you
* He's strong and independent
* He really seems to understand you

He's a zero . . . because he thinks it's cool to make jokes at other people's expense. He can be honest to the point of tactlessness and although he thinks his bizarre brand of humour is hilarious, very few people would agree. Plus . . .
* He can be cold and unfeeling sometimes
* He's a tad full of himself
* You never know where he is
* It's hard to know where he's going, where he's been or where he's coming from
* He's 100 per cent bonkers!

Personality Alert!
You may love him cracking jokes, but you'll soon go off it when you realize that he just won't stop!

He looks great . . . because, although he's not traditionally good-looking, he has an interesting and unusual face with wide-apart eyes, prominent cheekbones, a wide smiley mouth and a cute nose. When it comes to clothes, he has a rather distinctive style all of his own.

He's a state . . . *because* he's got a rather distinctive style all of his own!

Meet him . . .
– at the gym. (He likes to keep his lithe physique in peak condition – just in case he's called upon to save the world or something . . .)
– at the cinema, checking out the latest arty, subtitled film.
– collecting for charity. (So don't worry about going out looking for him – he'll be on your doorstep, rattling a collection box at you, before you know it!)

Impress him by . . . being cool and independent. The less girlie you are, the better. Mind you, he's a sucker for a bit of recognition so, when you first meet him, tell him you remember his fantastic performance in the Year 8 school play, and he'll be all yours! He has an intense dislike of soppy, overly romantic females, so forget the elaborately wrapped chocs and buy him a chip butty instead!

If you can't be bothered to do the running . . . he can run fast enough for you both. To get your attention, he'll do impressions, tickle you with his wit and "wisdom" and make a million silly faces. He'll also play practical jokes on you and rib you mercilessly. He'll ask loads of personal questions but won't tell you much in return. If you like a laugh-a-minute man of mystery, then Mr Aquarius is sure to win your heart!

Keep him by . . . not questioning his movements; tolerating his strange little "quirks"; putting up with his rowdy mates; never getting hysterical; not gossiping; smiling constantly.

Dump him when . . . he insists on making you the butt of all his awful jokes.

Love match: Gemini, Leo and Libra lasses just can't say no to him.

Top Aquarian totty: Robbie Williams.

Pisces (February 19–March 19)

He's a hero . . . because he's caring, helpful and, even as a mate, he'll always be there when you need him. As a boyfriend, he's really romantic, but that doesn't stop him from being a bit of a crazy party animal. Also . . .
* He's really loving

* He knows how to have a good time
* He's deep and philosophical
* He's always making romantic gestures
* He'll take you to fantasy-land (if you fancy it)
* He'd do anything for you

He's a zero . . . because his self-esteem is so low, it can be a drag always having to pump up his ego for him. Also, when it comes to practical stuff, he's just useless! (Q: How many Pisceans does it take to change a light bulb? A: Ten – nine to form a search party to go looking for a handyman and one to write a poem about it!) Plus . . .

* He's too scatty
* He doesn't know which way up he is
* He allows others to take advantage of him
* He's impressed by the dodgiest people
* He can't make a decision to save his life!

Personality Alert!

He's a dithering dreamer and you could get fed up constantly trying to pull his dappy little head out of the clouds.

He looks great . . . in second-hand clothes. He's got a really sweet face with large, watery-looking eyes, dimples, a long nose and a pouty mouth. His hair is baby-soft and tends to have a public schoolboy floppiness about it. He's got excellent posture (you'll never see a Piscean guy slouching), is naturally graceful (get him up on a catwalk!) and is a lovely little mover (see him go on that dance floor!). He likes comfy clothes in unusual styles and natural fabrics.

He's a state . . . when he tries to look smart: it's just not him!

Meet him . . .
- at a jumble sale or charity shop. (He may even work there.)
- at the local swimming baths or aquarium. (Pisces *is* the sign of the fish.)
- at a publishing house, trying to get them to publish his poems.

Impress him by . . . buying or making him a present and posting it to him. Once he gets the message that you fancy him, he'll ask you out. (So make sure he knows it's from you . . .) Once you get chatting to him, try not to be too argumentative – he hates confrontation; flatter him at every opportunity (telling him you dreamt about him is always a good chat-up line); and show him what a good listener you are. He loves that in a girl!

If you can't be bothered to do the running . . . he'll pursue you to the max. First, he'll try to impress you with his fancy footwork at the disco. If that doesn't work, he'll write you a song (and sing it to you too if you're "lucky"), send you flowers, and/or inundate you with love letters and other tokens of his affection. And he won't give up until you've at least acknowledged him (and his talents!)

Keep him by . . . analysing his dreams for him; kissing him a lot; having younger siblings or cousins (Piscean blokes love kids); remembering all your silly little anniversaries; not laughing when he sings to you; keeping a straight face when he talks about how you and he were together in a past life.

Dump him when . . . his love letters start making you feel bilious.

Love match: He's capable of loving forever – but only if you're a Cancerian, Virgoan or Scorpian girl.

Top Piscean totty: James Bradfield (Manic Street Preachers), Peter Andre, Jon Bon Jovi, Ronan Keating and Stephen Gately (Boyzone), Evan Dando and Graham Coxon (Blur).

Love Match

Check our specially devised compatibility chart over the page and discover whether or not you and the boy of your dreams are destined to be celestial soul-mates . . .

LOVE MATCH COMPATIBILITY CHART

IF HE'S ▶ AND YOU'RE ▼	ARIES	TAURUS	GEMINI	CANCER	LEO
PISCES					
ARIES					
TAURUS					
GEMINI					
CANCER					
LEO					
VIRGO					
LIBRA					
SCORPIO					
SAGITTARIUS					
CAPRICORN					
AQUARIUS					

First find your own compatibility symbo

en discover what it says about you and your star boy . . .

Making It Work

This system revolves around the elements. First find out which element you are by checking out your own symbol on the compatibility chart.

If the symbols for your sign are – ⚡ 🍬 🐞 or 🐚 – you're **Miss Fire**, which means you:
- Are passionate, flirtatious and excitable
- Love a challenge
- Are outgoing and confident in most situations
- Can be nasty
- Would rather snog than talk!
- Find it hard to say "no"
- Are adventurous, daring and would try anything once
- Never hold back your emotions
- Don't take life too seriously

If the symbols for your sign are – 🌻 🚲 ⚽ or 🍸 – you're **Miss Earth**, which means you:
- Are sexy but subtle
- Are sensual, sensitive and very touchy-feely
- Are down-to-earth, hard-working, practical and reliable
- Have a great sense of humour
- Love all the good things in life
- Can be bossy

- Hate anyone saying "no" to you
- Could never be unfaithful
- Take love and life pretty seriously

If the symbols for your sign are – ⚭ ● ❦ or ☔ – you're **Miss Air**, which means you:
- Love a good gossip
- Can be a bit cool
- Have the ability to see people as they really are
- Are always on the phone
- Are childlike and uninhibited.
- Have trouble being faithful in a relationship
- Tend to speak your mind
- Love the thrill of the romantic chase
- Like to be logical, rational and controlled (even when some emotion is called for)

If the symbols for your sign are – 🜚 ⚱ 〽 or 🜛 – you're **Miss Water**, which means you:
- Are incredibly romantic
- Are sensitive to the needs, moods and feelings of others
- Need a lot of love, attention and affection
- Can be moody
- Have a fantastic imagination
- Don't mind someone else taking the lead in most situations
- Like art and literature
- Can be talked into doing things you'd rather not do at all
- Are a bit secretive

Now you know which element you are, discover what you can do to make the relationship between you and your chosen bloke a success. Check the symbol for you and your star boy on the compatibility chart, and read on . . .

What a red-hot combination this is! As two fiery Fire signs, this relationship is wild. The main trouble is though that as you're both so lusty, there's no way either of you can contain your desire for passing fancies and are unlikely to be able to stay the course. If either of you decide that you want to get serious, this fiery coupling will burn itself out fairly sharpish. Even if you stay together for the passion, it's unlikely to go on forever: no one (not even someone as passionate as you) can stand *that* much heat!

Make it work by . . .
. . . At least *trying* to stay faithful
. . . Slowing down and realizing that love isn't a race or a competition
. . . Showing your soft side now and again – and that applies to both of you

As a Fire sign, you're a pretty realistic person and although you're enthusiastic when it comes to love, you don't have too many expectations about this romance. This Earth bloke has both feet firmly planted on the ground and, although you can be steady when you want to be, you may not want to be with *this* bloke, who may prove to be a bit of a drag in the long term. While you're lively and impulsive, he's sedate and cautious and sure to put a damper on any of your bright spark ideas. If you do end up together, then it has a reasonable chance of succeeding, but only if you can keep things interesting.

Make it work by . . .

. . . Making more of an effort to appreciate his sensible side (instead of ridiculing it)

. . . Telling him not to expect you to do all the work — especially when it comes to keeping the relationship alive

. . . Not forcing him to talk when he doesn't want to

His Airy personality may fan your Fire-y one, and although he may have a calming effect on you on one level, it may not make for much excitement. When you first meet, you're likely to be bowled over by his flirtatious charm, and a romance could flare up pretty quickly. He's a bit moody though, and the way he blows hot and cold is perhaps something you may not be able to handle. Generally, he allows you to take the lead and he's happy to do whatever you want, but your demands may prove too much for him in the end.

Make it work by . . .
. . . Being less demanding
. . . Not getting wound up by the things he says and
does
. . . Remembering his needs as well as your own

You're Fire; he's Water. You're hot; he's cool. This
doesn't mean he's not passionate – he is, but in a very
gentle, romantic way. He's fairly traditional by nature
and you shock him with your rather forceful
personality. And whereas you like romance to be a bit
of a laugh, he's deadly serious about it. If you're keen
to make a go of this relationship, you may have trouble
keeping the fires of passion burning past a certain
point. But he's adaptable and willing to learn. And who
better to teach him than you?

Make it work by . . .
. . . Appreciating and accepting your differences
. . . Taking him in hand
. . . Helping him look on the bright side of life

If you two get together – and you will because,
although you're different in so many ways (you're an
Earth sign and he's Fire), you share some basic
qualities and interests – what may concern you most

is his apparent lack of concern for you. You may look up to him at first, but as your relationship progresses, you realize that he may not be as romantic as you'd initially envisaged him to be. And because you like to be shown a lot of tenderness, this could bother you and could even put you off him. If you can give him the space and inspiration he requires, the flames of passion between you are capable of reaching great heights.

Make it work by . . .
. . . Teaching him how to be more caring
. . . Not placing him on a pedestal
. . . Giving him room to breathe within the relationship

What many might envisage to be a rather safe, possibly unexciting relationship, could easily become a rewarding and emotionally satisfying partnership. You're both Earth signs – gritty, practical and easy to read – and will have an instant liking for each other as soon as you meet. Together, you make a great team, warm and affectionate, each able to help the other free themselves from any insecurities. Because of this, your partnership should succeed.

Make it work by . . .
. . . Not letting others put you off each other
. . . Giving each other almost constant support and encouragement

. . . Not allowing jealousy or possessiveness to come between you

When you first set eyes on him, he's like a breath of fresh air (and he would be – he's an Air sign). You're a solid Earth sign and, to him, represent a port in the storm of life . . . at the start anyway. Although he's charming and extremely sociable, his weird moods may bother you intensely, especially when one minute he's incredibly immature, and the next he's a man of the world. When it comes to love, you know what you like but your lack of spontaneity may bore him. Not that you're boring – far from it – but he needs such constant variety that only a girl with the most powerful imagination and energy could really make him hers. But if you're willing to work at it, it might just turn out OK.

Make it work by . . .
. . . Not expecting the relationship to work without either of you putting in any effort
. . . Being honest about what it is that bugs you both about each other
. . . Dealing with problems as and when they crop up

He needs a girl who's prepared to give him her all, and you may not be ready for all he's asking of you. You're

a realistic Earth sign and alarm bells start ringing for you even on your first date, when all he talks about is love and commitment. You may allow this to wash right over you (he *is* a mega-romantic Water sign, after all), and you find it hard to take such premature romantic rantings seriously. Romantically, he seems so experienced and this is what could make you fall for him. If he starts to believe his somewhat previous words of love, then he could easily fall for you too. This is a relationship that improves with age, so it may well be worth working at.

Make it work by ...
... Making your feelings known at all times
... Not throwing it all in at the first sign of trouble
... Remembering that he's just as sensitive as you are

You're a beautiful Airy-fairy and it's hardly surprising that he's initially attracted by your looks. Once he gets to know you, he'll appreciate your wicked sense of humour. He's mesmerized by your ever-changing needs and unpredictable nature, and although this may irritate the hell out of a less challenge-seeking guy, he finds everything about you quite charming. He's a mega-direct Fire sign and you like the way he says what he thinks. You also love his obvious delight in you and his fun-loving, impulsive character. Together, you're constantly changing and, although this could destroy many a relationship, yours will positively thrive on it.

Make it work by . . .
. . . Keeping him entertained
. . . Putting a stop to his constant demands
. . . Not worrying about what other people think

As an Air sign, your head's stuck in the clouds when it comes to love; as an Earth sign, his feet are firmly on the ground. You may not think this pairing could work, but it might . . . mainly because he could just provide you with the stability and security you need (and secretly crave). Having said that, it's unlikely that you fancy him immediately and he may have to prove himself before you'll give him the time of day. He's impressed by your sociable personality (slightly envious too, if the truth be known) and is so proud of you. It's only when you start to feel constrained by his emotional needs and believe your individuality is threatened that you start to panic. This relationship can only work if you make an extra-special effort.

Make it work by . . .
. . . Being more realistic about your relationship
. . . Not expecting so much all the time
. . . Maintaining your independence

Air signs love a chat and when you two Airy types get

together, there's a whole lot of yakking going on! In fact, you talk so much, it's surprising if there's any time left for anything else! You realize pretty quickly how alike you are mentally, and because of this, you may be reluctant to spoil things by getting romantically embroiled. For those who *do* get involved, however, there are surprises that are well worth waiting for. Variety is the spice of your love life and you're both happy to go out of your way to work out new ways of having fun. A good pairing all in all.

Make it work by . . .
. . . Talking less and doing more
. . . Not being scared to admit your feelings for each other
. . . Keeping your romance exciting

You're attracted by his quiet, almost mysterious aura and he's charmed by your easy-going and friendly ways. You both possess a great sense of fun (you especially as a cheeky Air sign) and this is what brings you together ultimately. You're likely to have a great time too, although his regular bouts of insecurity and the fact that you never seem to want to do anything at the same time can bug you at times. His emotions run deep (and they would – he's a Water sign), but in the long term might cause far too many ripples in the relationship for your liking.

Make it work by . . .

. . . Making him feel secure (and that means no more
flirting with other boys!)

. . . Getting your body clocks in sync

. . . Not taking responsibility for his happiness

He's a Fire sign and you're attracted to his warm glow,
but no matter how hard you try to make him warm to
you, you'll soon have him raging. Because you're so
different from him, he sees you as a challenge and will
do his utmost to ruffle your cool surface. With regards
to love and romance, you're quite different, with him
being far more passionate than you. If you're one of the
more feisty Water signs, you may feel you've met your
match, but don't think for a second that you've got any
hold over him: he's his own person and if you try to pin
him down, the whole thing could get out of control,
ending in you getting seriously burnt.

Make it work by . . .

. . . Stopping winding each other up on purpose

. . . Being a bit more laid-back

. . . Looking on the bright side a bit more often

Although you're a Water sign and he's Earth, you're

similar in many ways and are naturally attracted to each other. You may be disappointed to find though, as time goes on, that he can be a bit of a tiresome stick-in-the-mud who doesn't appreciate your impetuous side. Nevertheless, he can provide you with comfort, stability and security; and you can help him to grow in every direction. If you can put up with the way he allows everyday life to interfere with your relationship, and if he can understand that you're not quite as practical as he is, then this relationship might be worth following through.

Make it work by . . .
. . . Understanding that you'll never really see eye to eye on certain matters
. . . Appreciating his bad points
. . . Letting him know when you're upset

His charm captivates you, but you can't understand why he finds it so hard to have eyes only for you. As a restless Air sign, he wants constant variety, and this may be a whim you're disinclined to entertain. In your opinion, he's a bit mad and, although you may find this exciting at first, you'll soon be wondering when he's going to start behaving "normally". Chances are, he won't. And when he realizes that as a commitment-keen Water sign you're after more than just a good time, he might fly off.

Make it work by . . .
. . . Not trying to change him
. . . Chilling out a bit
. . . Not swamping him with emotional demands

As two Water signs, your thoughts and feelings flow together naturally, and in theory you should get on fine. You both like to take the lead in love, but because you're both so sensitive, problems could arise. You're also both very possessive – him more so – and jealousy could cause many rows. On the up side, he can make you feel desirable and he feels you really understand him; if you want to make a go of it, you could form a very deep bond. But it won't be easy, that's for certain . . .

Make it work by . . .
. . . Taking it in turns to be boss
. . . Talking through any worries you have about your relationship
. . . Really *wanting* it to work

The Venus Effect

Discover where love planet Venus was on the day you were born and your romantic personality will be revealed . . .

Look to the list below to find out which sign Venus was in on your birth day . . .

<u>Birth date</u>	*Venus was in . . .*
1979	
Jan 1–6	Scorpio
Jan 7–Feb 4	Sagittarius
Feb 5–Mar 3	Capricorn
Mar 4–28	Aquarius
Mar 29–Apr 22	Pisces
Apr 23–May 17	Aries
May 18–Jun 11	Taurus
Jun 12–Jul 5	Gemini
Jul 6–31	Cancer
Aug 1–23	Leo
Aug 24–Sep 16	Virgo
Sep 17–Oct 10	Libra
Oct 11–Nov 3	Scorpio
Nov 4–28	Sagittarius
Nov 29–Dec 22	Capricorn
Dec 23–31	Aquarius

Birth date	Venus was in . . .
1980	
Jan 1–15	Aquarius
Jan 16–Feb 9	Pisces
Feb 10–Mar 6	Aries
Mar 7–Apr 3	Taurus
Apr 4–May 12	Gemini
May 13–Jun 4	Cancer
Jun 5–Aug 6	Gemini
Aug 7–Sep 7	Cancer
Sep 8–Oct 4	Leo
Oct 5–29	Virgo
Oct 30–Nov 23	Libra
Nov 24–Dec 17	Scorpio
Dec 18–31	Sagittarius
1981	
Jan 1–10	Sagittarius
Jan 11–Feb 3	Capricorn
Feb 4–27	Aquarius
Feb 28–Mar 23	Pisces
Mar 24–Apr 17	Aries
Apr 18–May 11	Taurus
May 12–Jun 4	Gemini
Jun 5–29	Cancer
Jun 30–Jul 24	Leo
Jul 25–Aug 18	Virgo
Aug 19–Sep 12	Libra
Sep 13–Oct 8	Scorpio
Oct 9–Nov 5	Sagittarius
Nov 6–Dec 8	Capricorn
Dec 9–31	Aquarius

Birth date

1982

Jan 1–22	Aquarius
Jan 23–Mar 1	Capricorn
Mar 2–Apr 6	Aquarius
Apr 7–May 4	Pisces
May 5–30	Aries
May 31–Jun 25	Taurus
Jun 26–Jul 20	Gemini
Jul 21–Aug 13	Cancer
Aug 14–Sep 7	Leo
Sep 8–Oct 1	Virgo
Oct 2–25	Libra
Oct 26–Nov 18	Scorpio
Nov 19–Dec 12	Sagittarius
Dec 13–31	Capricorn

Venus was in . . .

1983

Jan 1–5	Capricorn
Jan 6–29	Aquarius
Jan 30–Feb 22	Pisces
Feb 23–Mar 18	Aries
Mar 19–Apr 12	Taurus
Apr 13–May 8	Gemini
May 9–Jun 5	Cancer
Jun 6–Jul 9	Leo
Jul 10–Aug 26	Virgo
Aug 27–Oct 5	Leo
Oct 6–Nov 8	Virgo
Nov 9–Dec 6	Libra
Dec 7–31	Scorpio

Birth date	_Venus was in . . ._
1984	
Jan 1–25	Sagittarius
Jan 26–Feb 18	Capricorn
Feb 19–Mar 14	Aquarius
Mar 15–Apr 7	Pisces
Apr 8–May 1	Aries
May 2–26	Taurus
May 27–Jun 19	Gemini
Jun 20–Jul 13	Cancer
Jul 14–Aug 7	Leo
Aug 8–31	Virgo
Sep 1–25	Libra
Sep 26–Oct 19	Scorpio
Oct 20–Nov 13	Sagittarius
Nov 14–Dec 8	Capricorn
Dec 9–31	Aquarius
1985	
Jan 1–3	Aquarius
Jan 4–Feb 1	Pisces
Feb 2–Jun 5	Aries
Jun 6–Jul 5	Taurus
Jul 6–Aug 1	Gemini
Aug 2–28	Cancer
Aug 29–Sep 21	Leo
Sep 22–Oct 16	Virgo
Oct 17–Nov 9	Libra
Nov 10–Dec 3	Scorpio
Dec 4–26	Sagittarius
Dec 27–31	Capricorn

Birth date	**_Venus was in . . ._**

1986

Jan 1–19	Capricorn
Jan 20–Feb 12	Aquarius
Feb 13–Mar 8	Pisces
Mar 9–Apr 1	Aries
Apr 2–26	Taurus
Apr 27–May 21	Gemini
May 22–Jun 15	Cancer
Jun 16–Jul 11	Leo
Jul 12–Aug 7	Virgo
Aug 8–Sep 6	Libra
Sep 7–Dec 31	Scorpio

1987

Jan 1–6	Scorpio
Jan 7–Feb 4	Sagittarius
Feb 5–Mar 2	Capricorn
Mar 3–28	Aquarius
Mar 29–Apr 22	Pisces
Apr 23–May 16	Aries
May 17–Jun 10	Taurus
Jun 11–Jul 6	Gemini
Jul 7–29	Cancer
Jul 30–Aug 23	Leo
Aug 24–Sep 16	Virgo
Sep 17–Oct 10	Libra
Oct 11–Nov 3	Scorpio
Nov 4–27	Sagittarius
Nov 28–Dec 21	Capricorn
Dec 22–31	Aquarius

Birth date	**_Venus was in . . ._**
1988	
Jan 1–15	Aquarius
Jan 16–Feb 9	Pisces
Feb 10–Mar 5	Aries
Mar 6–Apr 3	Taurus
Apr 4–May 17	Gemini
May 18–26	Cancer
May 27–Aug 6	Gemini
Aug 7–Sep 6	Cancer
Sep 7–Oct 4	Leo
Oct 5–29	Virgo
Oct 30–Nov 23	Libra
Nov 24–Dec 17	Scorpio
Dec 18–31	Sagittarius
1989	
Jan 1–10	Sagittarius
Jan 11–Feb 3	Capricorn
Feb 4–27	Aquarius
Feb 28–Mar 23	Pisces
Mar 24–Apr 16	Aries
Apr 17–May 10	Taurus
May 11–Jun 4	Gemini
Jun 5–28	Cancer
Jun 29–Jul 23	Leo
Jul 24–Aug 17	Virgo
Aug 18–Sep 12	Libra
Sep 13–Oct 8	Scorpio
Oct 9–Nov 4	Sagittarius
Nov 5–Dec 9	Capricorn
Dec 10–31	Aquarius

Venus In Aries
Ups:

- You have a warm, loving nature
- You're always attractive to the opposite sex
- You have no fear about telling a boy if you fancy him
- You bring a lot of laughter into any relationship

Downs:

- You sometimes start rows just for the sheer hell of it
- You're not too good at choosing boyfriends, often ending up with someone totally unsuitable
- You don't find it easy to express your feelings
- You can be selfish

Venus In Taurus
Ups:

- Your love life is uncomplicated
- You're good-looking and charming
- You're affectionate and attentive
- You're sensual, considerate and faithful

Downs:

- Your tendency to be over-possessive and jealous can cause problems
- You can easily get into a romantic rut
- You have the potential to "waste" your love on someone quite undeserving
- You've got a fierce temper if you don't get what you want

Venus In Gemini
Ups:
- Guys can't get enough of you!
- You're ace at flirting
- You're really exciting company
- When love wanes, you find it easy to bounce back

Downs:
- You're easily bored and can end a potentially great romance because of that
- Your need to have two or three relationships simultaneously can get you into trouble
- You need constant mental stimulation (and, sadly, not many boys can provide that)
- You don't take other people's feelings seriously enough

Venus In Cancer
Ups:
- You're loyal, loving and lovable
- Your ever-changing moods make you very interesting company

- When you get the right sort of attention, you blossom into one of the sexiest girls around
- You always mean what you say – even though you don't always say what you mean . . .

Downs:
- You're a slave to your emotions
- You're a bit unrealistic about love
- You're too trusting at times

- You're so scared of being hurt, you'll avoid getting too close to anyone

Venus In Leo
Ups:
- You always stand out from the crowd
- You enjoy the whole process of forming relationships and love being in love
- You're generous, faithful and warm-hearted.
- You have the ability to make a boyfriend feel really special

Downs:
- You're so keen to be in a relationship, you rather rush into things and make loads of romantic mistakes
- Your sense of judgment isn't all that it should be
- You suffer more than your fair share of heartache
- You need loads of attention and don't always get it

Venus In Virgo
Ups:
- You are emotionally generous, always eager to please the one you love
- You're caring and thoughtful
- You're an exciting mixture of homely and sexy
- Because you're so intelligent and level-headed, you don't make too many mistakes on the love front

Downs:

- You can be inhibited
- You can be a bit of a mother hen with your boyfriend
- Your fussiness means you can go for long periods boyfriend-free
- You're all too easily put off by things that really don't matter

Venus In Libra

Ups:

- You're fun-loving and attractive
- You're extremely popular with the opposite sex and have no trouble charming the ones you fancy into submission
- You're sympathetic and fair-minded
- You always stay great mates with your exes

Downs:

- Your fear of hurting anyone's feelings means that you're just a girl who can't say no – and this gets you into all sorts of tricky situations
- Your love life is likely to be complicated
- Quite often, you fall in love just because you're in that sort of mood – and who the object of your affections might be is almost irrelevant
- You'd rather be with *anyone* than be alone

Venus In Scorpio

Ups:

- You can cope with any problems love throws at you

- You're passionate, intense and quite unforgettable
- When in love, you're incredibly loyal
- You're very sexy

Downs:

- You take love and life too seriously sometimes
- You often go for unavailable types
- Because of your obsessive tendencies, you run the risk of developing major, destination-nowhere crushes
- When a relationship ends, you can get nasty, particularly if you feel you've been wronged

Venus In Sagittarius

Ups:

- With your fantastic sense of humour and free-thinking ways, you're attractive to many members of the opposite sex
- In a relationship, you will enthral your partner with your fun-loving ways
- You're caring, warm and affectionate
- You're enthusiastic, energetic and communicative

Downs:

- As a naturally friendly and frank person, your openness is often taken the wrong way
- You need tons of freedom – something only a few boyfriends will be able to give you
- Your unpredictable behaviour baffles many a potential boyfriend
- You see love as some sort of game – and this can cause problems

Venus In Capricorn

Ups:

- You're persistent and always get your man, no matter how long it takes
- You have a talent for choosing great boyfriends
- You're faithful, loving and loyal
- Your great sense of humour makes you very attractive

Downs:

- You can be too cool sometimes, causing boys to see you as aloof and stand-offish
- You don't allow yourself to get deep enough into relationships to feel comfortable about expressing yourself
- Your great sense of logic often holds you back from getting involved in the first place
- Flirting doesn't come easy to you

Venus In Aquarius

Ups:

- You're physically very attractive and unquestionably cool
- You are always surrounded by admirers – even though you may be completely oblivious to them
- You're never short of potential boyfriends
- When you find someone who shares your outlook and understands your need for independence, you're an interesting and loyal partner

Downs:

- You can't differentiate between friendship and love and sometimes go out with someone who would have been best kept as a friend
- You fall in love far too easily
- You often make the mistake of trying to "change" boyfriends and most of them don't take kindly to this
- You tend to like a boy for what he *could* be rather than for what he is

Venus In Pisces

Ups:

- You're one of the most romantic signs of the zodiac
- You write the best love letters and have even been known to pen the odd love poem!
- You're attractive, compassionate and sensitive
- There's a queue of lads waiting to go out with you!

Downs:

- You have problems with jealousy, arising from your own insecurities
- You find it hard ending a relationship, even when you know it's not working
- You're waiting for Mr Perfect and don't seem to realize that he may not exist
- You make far too many sacrifices for boyfriends who don't deserve it

Part 4:

Friends And Rivals

Are You A Great Mate?

You can be the best friend in the world, mainly because you're just *sooo* kind and generous. Trouble is, you can be taken for granted and many so-called mates take advantage of you. Because you always like to see the best in people though, you rarely notice this; and it's only when their bad behaviour is pointed out to you that you realize what's going on and begin to feel hurt. Emotional attachment is vital to all Pisceans and you're no exception: when it comes to friendships, you often throw yourself in at the emotional deep end and get totally involved in the other person's life. This can be flattering for some but can be quite scary for others, especially when they've barely had the chance to introduce themselves! You can also be lacking in confidence and this could make you a tad difficult at times. This all makes you sound a bit heavy going and serious – and you *can* be – but in general you're a real fun person to have around: you have a great sense of humour, are always up for a laugh and are very sociable and friendly. You're also happy to think up fun things to do – although getting everything organized is another matter altogether and should ideally be left to someone else – a Capricorn mate most probably! Having said that, if no-one else is up for it, you'll happily give it your best shot. And although you're intense, you're not the sort of person who needs to see their mates every day: in fact, with most of your mates you're happy to go for relatively long periods of time without seeing them.

You make friends because you're:

- Unbiased and unprejudiced
- Always willing to listen
- A real laugh
- Happy to do all the organizing when it comes to nights out (even though you're not very good at it . . .)
- Kind, caring and generous
- Full of fab ideas

You lose friends because you're:

- A bit too much sometimes
- Very insecure
- Occasionally a bit offhand for no real reason
- As mad as the proverbial hatter
- Hard to keep track of
- Careless with phone numbers!!

Who's Your Friend?

You like people who can reassure, encourage and support you. Your self-esteem can sometimes be on the low side and you need mates who are happy (and naturally able) to boost your ego as and when it needs boosting. You need friends to organize you and take the lead in social situations. At the same time, you don't like to be overshadowed. Many Pisceans like their friends to be useful in some way. And you also like to be able to look up to them and admire them. From mates, you expect understanding, reassurance and undying loyalty. The best signs for friendship are – Cancer, Scorpio and other Pisceans. You sometimes get on well with your opposite sign of Virgo and are fond of Capricorns too. You don't like folk who don't make allowances for other people's weaknesses and aren't too keen on those who are as batty and scatty as you. Arien thoughtlessness bothers you; as does Geminian fickleness and Sagittarian carelessness.

Your Best Mate . . .

- Tells you you look gorgeous when you're having a bad hair day
- Would happily let you copy her homework
- Takes it in turns with you when "playing" princess and servant
- Is dead cool, good-looking and multitalented (but never flaunts it)
- Is loyal to the max (even after you let *her* down)
- Is probably an Earth or Water sign

The Other Signs As Friends

You've read all about what makes a Piscean friend. But what about the other eleven signs? Here's a list of their good and bad qualities . . .

Ariens . . .

. . . make great mates because they're:
- Warm
- Broadminded
- Generous
- Entertaining

. . . are dead-end friends because they're:
- Selfish
- Often inconsiderate
- Competitive
- Impatient

Taureans . . .

. . . make great mates because they're:
- Affectionate
- Reliable
- Strong
- Trustworthy

. . . are dead-end friends because they're:
- Possessive

- A bit dismissive of any form of weakness
- Tactless
- Snobby

Geminians . . .

. . . make great mates because they're:

- Spontaneous
- Helpful
- Tons of fun
- Amusing

. . . are dead-end friends because they're:

- Never on time
- Prone to fibbing
- Fickle
- Unpredictable

Cancerians . . .

. . . make great mates because they're:

- Kind
- Hospitable
- Sensitive
- Loyal

. . . are dead-end friends because they're:

- Hypersensitive
- Prone to bearing grudges – for ages!
- Judgmental
- Clingy

Leos . . .

. . . make great mates because they're:

- Great fun
- Generous
- Proud of you
- Loving

. . . are dead-end friends because they're:
- Easily upset
- Likely to ignore you for no apparent reason
- Hard to get to know properly
- A bit pig-headed

Virgoans . . .
. . . make great mates because they're:
- Fussy about who they're friends with. (If you're a Virgoan's mate, count yourself privileged!)
- Refined
- Considerate
- Keen to help in any way they can

. . . are dead-end friends because they're:
- Hypercritical
- Terrible worriers
- A bit sarky sometimes
- Always right (or *think* they are anyway . . .)

Librans . . .
. . . make great mates because they're:
- Loving and lovable
- Honest
- Fair
- Gentle

. . . are dead-end friends because they're:

- *Sooo* indecisive
- Occasionally jealous (especially of mates who are prettier than them)
- A bit grumpy sometimes
- Very sulky (especially if you neglect them for any period of time)

Scorpians . . .

. . . make great mates because they're:

- Absolutely hilarious
- Really generous
- Always make you feel welcome (even when you call round at the worst possible moment!)
- Will never gossip about you (no matter what juicy morsels you entrust them with!)

. . . are dead-end friends because they're:

- Lazy about getting in touch
- Even lazier about answering the phone (especially if they've got an answerphone to do it for them)
- Able to read your mind
- Liable to turn nasty if you upset them

Sagittarians . . .

. . . make great mates because they're:

- Sociable
- Always willing to stick up for their mates (even if they don't really agree with them)
- Honest
- Open-minded

... are dead-end friends because they're:

- *Too* honest sometimes (some would call it totally tactless)
- Prone to temper tantrums
- Occasionally violent and abusive – verbally and physically
- Unable to keep a secret

Capricornians ...

... make great mates because they're:

- Happy to stick by their nearest and dearest through thick and thin
- Sincere
- Wildly generous when it comes to their mates' birthdays
- Ever so kind (when they want to be)

... are dead-end friends because they're:

- Terrible judges of character
- Quite vicious if they're rejected in any way
- Unnecessarily suspicious of everyone and sometimes test their friends – just to see how loyal they are
- Users – or are capable of using a mate to get something (or someone) they want

Aquarians ...

... make great mates because they're:

- Intelligent and interesting
- Happy to make a lot of effort when it comes to staying in touch with friends
- Not bothered about being woken up at four in the

morning to help a friend in need (most of the time anyway . . .)

• Majorly friendly and sociable

. . . are dead-end friends because they're:

• Inclined to want everyone – mates especially – to live by their own rather high standards
• Always stealing your ideas
• Desperate to be the boss in all relationships
• Occasionally self-centred, in that sometimes they believe their problems are more important than anyone else's

Forever Friends?

Now you've got the general idea of what all the separate signs are like, check the friendship chart over the page to find out more about friendship compatibility . . .

There's an astrological theory about friendship which revolves around the order of the signs. To discover how it works, take a look at the chart on the next page, find your sign down the side and your friends' signs along the top, make a note of the symbol where the two signs meet, then check the "key" panel below. This should give you a good indication of how you and your mates get on . . .

Friendship Chart

Your sign ▼ \ Your friend's sign ▶	Aries	Taurus	Gemini	Cancer	Leo	Virgo	Libra	Scorpio	Sagittarius	Capricorn	Aquarius	Pisces
Pisces	※	❀	▦	✿	❁	◙	⊕	❋	❖	◎	✾	◉
Aries	◉	※	❀	▦	✿	❁	◙	⊕	❋	❖	◎	✾
Taurus	✾	◉	※	❀	▦	✿	❁	◙	⊕	❋	❖	◎
Gemini	◎	✾	◉	※	❀	▦	✿	❁	◙	⊕	❋	❖
Cancer	❖	◎	✾	◉	※	❀	▦	✿	❁	◙	⊕	❋
Leo	❋	❖	◎	✾	◉	※	❀	▦	✿	❁	◙	⊕
Virgo	⊕	❋	❖	◎	✾	◉	※	❀	▦	✿	❁	◙
Libra	◙	⊕	❋	❖	◎	✾	◉	※	❀	▦	✿	❁
Scorpio	❁	◙	⊕	❋	❖	◎	✾	◉	※	❀	▦	✿
Sagittarius	✿	❁	◙	⊕	❋	❖	◎	✾	◉	※	❀	▦
Capricorn	▦	✿	❁	◙	⊕	❋	❖	◎	✾	◉	※	❀
Aquarius	❀	▦	✿	❁	◙	⊕	❋	❖	◎	✾	◉	※

Key:

◎ – If you and a friend are the same sign – Pisces in this instance – you're too similar. You can be friends, but because you're so aware of each other's failings, you're likely to drive each other mad and need to be extra tolerant.

✳ – If you make friends with a person who is one sign ahead of you – as an Piscean, this would be an Arien – they're very different from you, but are in possession of many of the qualities that you aspire to have. This person is a real example to you, is able to teach you many things (if you're prepared to learn, that is), and can lead you from where you are now in life to the next stage. But, because of your obvious differences, you're unlikely to be best mates.

✺ – A friend whose sign is the one before yours – Aquarius in your case – may appear to be radically different from you on the surface, but has a great understanding of your innermost fears and desires. They're a good person to fall back on in times of trouble, as they can listen without being judgmental. But, if you go out socializing together, you're unlikely to have that great a time. (That's if you can even agree on where you are going to go and what you are going to do in the first place!)

◉ – Someone two signs ahead of you – and for you, as a Piscean, this would be a Taurean – is a person you're really comfortable with. This person is almost like a brother or sister to you: you're able to spend a lot of time in their company (in fact, many friends two signs apart can even live together quite happily), but this relationship won't be as exciting as others you might have. This mate is mega-loyal though, will always be there for you, so is well worth hanging on to.

❀ – A friend whose sign is two signs behind yours – a Capricornian in your case – is capable of being a great mate. You may not have an overwhelming need to see a lot of each other, but when you do you're sure to have a fine time. It's unlikely that you'll ever get *really* close to this person, but stick with them and they'll prove what a good friend they can be time and time again.

❁ – If your friend is three signs ahead of you – and as a Piscean, that would make them a Geminian – you could find them rather difficult. Not difficult enough to put you off wanting to spend time with them, but more of a challenge. You have differing views on almost everything, but this just makes for plenty of heated debate. Occasionally, this person really gets on your nerves, but for the most part you find them *kind* of entertaining.

❃ – If you have a friend whose sign is three signs behind yours – a mate who's a Sagittarian in your case, Miss Pisces – you may not be on the most intimate terms, but they often feel obliged to help you. You don't have an emotional or spiritual link with this person, but may see eye to eye on other matters – work, maybe;

money, perhaps. They're the sort of friend you can rely on for sensible advice and are able to point you in the right direction on a practical level. But they have to be in the right frame of mind to do it . . .

✿ – If you've befriended an individual who is four signs ahead of you **or** four signs behind you – a Cancerian or a Scorpian in your case – you share the same element (Water, in this case) and are likely to have tons in common. Sometimes, you can feel envious of them, especially the friend who is four signs ahead of you (Cancer) and you may long to be as talented as they are. On the other hand, they can be a real inspiration to you, firing your ambitions and giving you lots of ideas, but if you spend too much time together, the envy could get the better of you in the end . . .

⊕ – A friend who's five signs ahead of you – and for you, Pisces, that would be a Leo – is *capable* of helping you get to where you want to be, but may not *want* to help you. Not much of a mate at all really . . .

✤ – Someone five signs behind you – a Libran in your case – is so very alien to you, but there's something about them that you find interesting. It's not that you have anything in common with this person – you're like chalk and cheese – but you have a strange kind of respect for the way they run their life. Even though you don't understand much of their behaviour, for some reason you just can't help being mesmerized by them. Weird, or what?

◉ – Your opposite sign or the sign that's six signs ahead of or behind your own – Virgo in your case, Pisces – will be naturally attracted to you and, to start with, you may believe that you have a lot in common. On the surface it seems that way, but once you get to know each other you realize just how different you are. This can lead to conflict but more often than not it makes for an exciting (though unpredictable) friendship. You are different on every level – physical, intellectual and emotional – and, while this can be a pain sometimes, ultimately you seem to complement each other and get on just fine.

With Friends Like That . . .

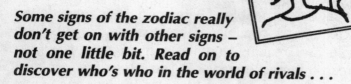

Some signs of the zodiac really don't get on with other signs – not one little bit. Read on to discover who's who in the world of rivals . . .

As a **Piscean**, you like a laugh. So do **Leos**. The trouble is, neither sign finds the other that funny, so laughs would be seriously lacking if you ever got together. Pisceans often find themselves *mildly* amused by **Geminians**, but once within twenty paces of each other, much rubbing up the wrong way begins. The people you Pisceans should really make an effort to avoid are **Librans** and **Sagittarians** – neither sign is nasty by nature, but there's something about a sweet little Piscean that brings out the sadist in them. So watch out! (Unless you're a glutton for punishment, that is . . .)

And the other signs?

Aries

Ariens may have a lot of mates but, if the truth be known, they don't actually like many people at all. Which is strange because, all in all, they're pretty popular themselves. The people they dislike most tend to be fellow **Ariens**, **Cancerians** and **Virgoans**. If they get hate mail, it *may* be from an Arien, but it's more likely to be sent by a **Scorpian** or **Capricornian**, who aren't overly keen on rams at all.

Taurus

Taureans are likeable sorts, and would have you believe that they are incapable of being nasty. But, deep down, they're just as capable as anyone else of upsetting people and making enemies. The sign that bugs a Taurean the most however is **Leo** – they just *can't* get on; and, although **Librans** are ruled by the same planet as Taurus (Venus), that's about all they've got in common. They're unlikely to receive hate mail from these people though – mainly because it's **Sagittarians** and **Aquarians** who are Taurus' worst enemies . . . They just don't understand Taureans at all and that worries them silly.

Gemini

Geminians are friendly and give most people the benefit of the doubt. Everybody except virtuous **Virgoans** that is, who, although ruled by planet Mercury (the same planet that rules Gemini), are a right royal pain in the butt to slightly immoral Gemini! **Scorpio** folk aren't too popular with Geminians either: they're just *soooo* infuriating! (In Gemini's opinion anyway.) But any poison pen letters that land on a Geminian's doormat are most likely to have been sent by a **Capricornian** (who finds Gemini's ways immensely aggravating) or a **Piscean** (who could be just plain jealous).

Cancer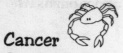

Cancerians sometimes seem to hate everyone – they get *that* grumpy! The people they consistently dislike are **Librans** and **Sagittarians**. Librans are so blimmin' wishy-washy (in Cancer's opinion) and Sagittarians don't seem to have anything in common with Cancer at all. Which is strange, because Libra and Sagittarius don't have too many problems with Cancer. But it's **Aquarians** and **Ariens** who find Cancerians the most bugsome. Such is life, eh?

Leo

Leos aren't overly keen on **Scorpians** (for a myriad of reasons) and **Capricornians** (who seem only to be friendly to Leo when they want something). In return though, Scorpio tries to lean on Leo on occasion and Capricorn kind of looks up to them, but that doesn't really interest Leo. Real rivals aren't these folk at all though: Leos should watch out for **Taureans** and you **Pisceans** – you're the ones out to get 'em! Yikes!

Virgo

Virgoans are right old fusspots and, because they're so picky when it comes to mates, should sometimes count themselves lucky to have any mates at all! The people who peeve them the most are **Sagittarians** and **Aquarians**: Virgo has no use for them at all. But real enemies come in the form of **Ariens** and **Geminians** – they've *really* got it in for Virgo.

Libra

Librans are real sweethearts but that doesn't stop them disliking people from time to time. They're generally patient types but can, on occasion, get irritated. Top offenders, in Libra's eyes, are **Capricornians** and **Pisceans** – you folk are such a pain! But if anyone's going to boil a Libran's bunny, it'll be a **Taurean** or a **Cancerian**. They might *seem* soft, but when they get riled, they get *really* riled. (And sometimes all it takes is a Libran getting in their way.)

Scorpio

Scorpios are sometimes a tad paranoid and need trustworthy types as mates; that's why a rowdy **Arien** or a blabbermouth **Aquarian** wouldn't do as a mate at all. It's a shame, because those two signs are really quite fond of Scorpio. In fact, Miss Scorpio would be seriously surprised to discover who'd be most likely to hide sardines in her curtain pole: it'd be none other than a crazy **Gemini** or a mad **Leo**. Who'd have thought it, eh?

Sagittarius

Sagittarians like a laugh so wouldn't be seen dead with

a stick-in-the-mud **Taurean** or a moochy old **Piscean** (Saggie's opinion only!). A Sagittarian would be more inclined to seek out the company of a **Cancerian** or a **Virgoan**, which is a shame because *they'd* probably turn Saggie down, due to the fact that they find them really annoying . . . Sad but true.

Capricorn

Capricornians need friends, but they will not tolerate **Ariens** or **Geminians** under any circumstances. Not that these signs would cause them any harm – as you know, Aries and Gemini types don't actually pay too much attention to Capricorns at all. The people Capricornians should steer well clear of – and who could, if they wanted to, do untold damage to a Capricorn's reputation – are **Leos** (who find Caps immensely dull) and **Librans** (who won't even spare them the time of day).

Aquarius

Aquarians like excitement but, in their opinion, that's not something they'll get from ploddy old **Taureans** and depressing old **Cancerians**. Not that these folk are particularly nasty to Aquarius. Oh no. Real enemies come in the guise of vicious (and they *can* be when the mood takes them) **Virgoans** and spiteful **Scorpians**: they're the ones who'll plant cress seeds in your carpet and water it while you're on holiday . . .

Part 5:

Home And Family

Pisces At Home

So long as the people you live with understand that you're a sensitive, emotional kind of person – and make allowances for this – then you're probably a joy to live with.

Your Room

You're a bit of a hippy really, aren't you? And nowhere is this better reflected than in your room. It's like entering a comfy, welcoming Aladdin's cave. Yes, it's cluttered but it's fascinating clutter – old photos; rare books; unusual and striking paintings and prints of seascapes or religious scenes, spiritual items – Buddhas, Hindu statues, Moslem artefacts; unusual items of clothing on display – a Japanese kimono, for instance, or a Peruvian shawl . . . There are also likely to be odd sketches drawn by friends or family stuck on the walls, which, incidentally, will probably be papered in some unusual design. You also like plants and flowers to be prominent, and no surprises if there's a fish tank, too. Being a fishy sort yourself (fish being the Piscean symbol), you probably want to be surrounded by your own kind! So much stuff makes it sound like there'd be no room to swing a catfish, but somehow your room will seem surprisingly spacious. You're probably fascinated by the ancient art of Feng Shui but can never get organised enough to actually rearrange all your stuff as per the rules.

Ideally, your floors will be wooden and rug-topped and you may have bamboo or paper blinds hanging at your windows. There are likely to be scatter cushions and beanbags on the floor as this is where you prefer to sit – your guests are welcome to the bed. These days, your dolphin quilt cover has gone: instead you've opted for unusual bed linen in sumptuous fabrics. Finally, colours . . . Pisceans feel at home with all shades of blue and green, but occasionally go for something more dramatic in shades of purple and red.

Happy Families?

Your family are massively important to you. You're in constant need of their love and support. It's also important for them to understand just how emotional and sensitive you are. It's vital that you're treated as an individual. The star signs of family members have great bearing on how you get on. There's an astrological theory that if you're one of the "masculine" signs (i.e. Aries, Gemini, Leo, Libra, Sagittarius or Aquarius), you'll be most influenced throughout your childhood by your dad; and if your star sign is "feminine" (Taurus, Cancer, Virgo, Scorpio, Capricorn or Pisces), then you're more likely to be influenced by your mum. As a Piscean, you'll probably find it's your mum who exerts the most power over you.

You And Your Parents*

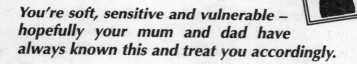

You're soft, sensitive and vulnerable – hopefully your mum and dad have always known this and treat you accordingly.

You and an **Arien** dad? Mmmmm, risky. He's loud, tactless, insensitive and impatient – not the kind of man who's likely to understand you. Things will work out a little better with your Arien mum: she's short-tempered but more understanding.

You'll probably appreciate **Taurean** parents because they tend to be protective kind of folk. They may not be the most imaginative people though, so be prepared for Taurean mum or dad to scoff at your special psychic abilities.

Like you, a **Geminian** mum or dad may be artistic, but the similarity ends here. Geminian mum drives you mad because she's just so flippant about everything, and Geminian dad may irritate you with the shallow comments he thinks are so funny.

Caring **Cancerian** mum will give you all the loving you need and provide you with a safe, secure home. Cancerian dad is the perfect dad for you – he's just so sensitive and understanding.

'Fraid it's unlikely you'll see eye to eye with feisty **Leo** mum. While she's madly enthusiastic about life, it seems like you have more sensitivity in your little finger

*If you don't live with your parents, consider the star signs of your guardian/s or main carer/s instead.

than she has in her whole body. But Leo dad's such a showman, it's unlikely you'll be able to resist him.

Virgoan parents are likely to be loving and interested but they're probably too practical for you truly to connect. Virgoan mum's likely to be overcritical at times, while Virgoan dad can seem rather emotionless.

Libran mum's probably just about perfect for you. She's easy-going and sensitive and won't allow you to get too down. Libran dad's likely to be a thoroughly charming individual but there may be times when you wish he'd save it all for you.

While she can be strict, there's no doubting that emotional **Scorpian** mum understands her little fish. Of course she does, she's a Water sign like you. Scorpian dad may seem a little scary at times, but it's worth remembering that he's sensitive, too.

Sagittarian dad will embarrass you with his daft practical jokes, while you may well resent the time Sagittarian mum gives to her numerous causes and interests. You need her more than anyone.

Capricornian dad may be loving but he probably finds it difficult to show you. Capricornian mum is patient and makes you feel secure but why does she have to be so critical?

Like you, **Aquarians** have something of a "dreamy" reputation so it's likely you'll get on OK with an Aquarian mum or dad.

It's a meeting of minds between you and your **Piscean** parent. Piscean dad will be super-sensitive and understanding. If you have any complaint about a Piscean mum it's probably that she and you are too alike!

Any Brothers Or Sisters?

Family is really important to you so it's likely you rate your brothers and sisters, providing they're your kind of people (i.e. sensitive, understanding, artistic and emotional). If they're not, then you may find it rather difficult to relate to them. There's a danger that a more forthright brother or sister will dominate you. which may end up with you feeling rather squashed. So which star sign suits you best as a sister or brother?

Although you're very different, you probably get on with your **Arien sister**, particularly if she's younger than you. She may get impatient at times, but she'll be fascinated by the wild and wacky stories you tell her. An **Arien brother**, whether older or younger, may well be too gung-ho for you.

While you probably appreciate the kindness of your **Taurean sister**, you're actually not really very much alike. However, **Taurean brother** could teach you to stand up for your beliefs and not be swayed and could make a top sibling.

You'll admire the lightning wit of a **Geminian sibling**, but you may be scornful of a sister in particular because she never seems to feel things deeply. You'll wish your **Geminian brother** was more reliable.

Your **Cancerian sibling** will be almost as emotional

as you are and always sympathetic and willing to listen. However, they're not very good at lifting you out of a mood when you're feeling low.

A **Leo brother** and you? You're likely to be blown away by his exuberance! Your bossy, oh-so-confident **Leo sister** may make you feel inadequate at times.

Your **Virgoan brother** or **sister** may annoy you with their perfectionism and bossiness.

Your **Libran sibling** loves harmony, so you're unlikely to fall out with them. There may be times, however, when you secretly despise them: how can they remain so calm when you're freaking out?

You'll admire your older **Scorpian sister's** great determination to do what she wants. Your **Scorpian brother's** probably just as emotional as you are.

Sagittarian lack of tact doesn't go down terribly well with you. Why can't your Sagittarian sibling think before opening their mouth?

You know you can rely on a safe, steady **Capricornian brother** or **sister**, but you wish they had more of an imagination. They're just so sensible!

You'll enjoy listening to your **Aquarian siblings'** rather eccentric ideas about life, love and the universe. They'll really fire up your imagination. But they always think they're right – and how annoying is that?

Of course, you'll be on the same wavelength as your **Piscean sibling**. The only problem is that both older and younger sibs are prone to moodiness and this could cause friction.

If you want to find out more about compatibility within your family, check out the chart opposite . . .

Are you compatible with your family? Check out this destiny chart and find out . . .

Your Sign	Your perfect mum is . . .	Your perfect dad is . . .	Mum from hell is . . .	Dad from hell is . . .	Best brother is . . .	Best sister is . . .
PISCES	Libra or Scorpio	Pisces or Cancer	Leo	Aries	Taurus	Aries
ARIES	Aries or Leo	Libra or Sagittarius	Virgo	Pisces	Gemini	Taurus
TAURUS	Taurus or Virgo	Scorpio or Capricorn	Gemini	Sagittarius	Cancer	Gemini
GEMINI	Aries or Sagittarius	Gemini or Aquarius	Pisces	Taurus	Leo	Cancer
CANCER	Cancer or Libra	Pisces or Taurus	Sagittarius	Aquarius	Virgo	Leo
LEO	Aries or Cancer	Scorpio or Aquarius	Libra	Capricorn	Libra	Virgo
VIRGO	Cancer or Virgo	Capricorn or Taurus	Aries	Leo	Scorpio	Libra
LIBRA	Gemini or Libra	Aries or Aquarius	Scorpio	Cancer	Sagittarius	Scorpio
SCORPIO	Scorpio or Pisces	Taurus or Capricorn	Cancer	Gemini	Capricorn	Sagittarius
SAGITTARIUS	Gemini or Aquarius	Aries or Leo	Taurus	Scorpio	Aquarius	Capricorn
CAPRICORN	Taurus or Capricorn	Virgo or Scorpio	Aquarius	Libra	Pisces	Aquarius
AQUARIUS	Gemini or Leo	Libra or Scorpio	Capricorn	Virgo	Aries	Pisces

Your Future Family

How many times you marry, the number of children you have and whether or not you'll have a happy family in the future all depends on your Sun Sign (Pisces) combined with your Rising Sign. Check out your Rising Sign (see pages 6–19), then check what it reveals below.

You're a Pisces with . . .

Aries Rising. You're a romance enthusiast. You fall in love with amazing regularity but spread yourself too thin. You may well marry early, in a hurry, but live to regret it – even though he's likely to be rich. You probably won't have many children or may decide against having them at all.

Taurus Rising. You're just an old-fashioned girl, aren't you? You long to fall in love with somebody who'll look after you. You'll probably find him – but guard against that jealous streak of yours. You'll have two or three kids.

Gemini Rising. You can't abide feeling tied down in a relationship so your husbands or life partners (and there'll probably be more than one) will have to give you a certain amount of freedom. Your children will be lucky and artistic and be an endless source of fascination to you.

Cancer Rising. You're an emotional rollercoaster. When you're up, you're in the clouds; when you're down, you're way down. You long for an equal relationship that brings the security you crave – you're just not happy being single. You'll marry once, possibly twice, and have kids from each relationship.

Leo Rising. You're impulsive but try to guard against this when it comes to love. You'll end up much happier if you take your time and wait till you're mature before settling down. Two marriages are likely with children from both unions. Twins are a possibility if you hook up with an Aquarian bloke.

Virgo Rising. You can't abide any kind of game playing in a relationship. Trust is the most important thing to you and when this is present with a partner, you're loving, loyal, honest and devoted. You'll marry once and have a smallish family.

Libra Rising. You look at love through rose-coloured specs, you're in love with the idea of being in love, but maybe you should be more realistic. You'll marry but there may be some kind of separation when you've been together for a while. However, your two or three children will be very lucky.

Scorpio Rising. You may pretend you're against

marriage but really you're not: as you're a bit insecure, you think it'll make you feel better. It looks like you'll marry more than once and have quite a big family. Twins or triplets are a possibility.

Sagittarius Rising. When young, you'll regard marriage as a bit of a trap. Although you may be tempted to settle down many times, it's doubtful you'll actually do it till you're older. Two or even three life partnerships seem likely. Children? It's unlikely there'll be more than two.

Capricorn Rising. You view love and romance in something of a practical way. Others instinctively trust you and once you give your heart, it tends to be for good. On the other hand, some with this combination find themselves marrying again and again. You'll have children and will be very ambitious for them.

Aquarius Rising. You're looking for a mate who'll provide companionship, communication and rapport. One thing is essential though – you'll need to feel free. When you do decide to settle down, it'll probably be for good. Your man may well be artistic and your children will be extremely happy.

Pisces Rising. Ideally, you'd never discard one partner for another – you'd keep the lot! Sounds great in theory but in reality it's not possible. You will marry eventually (more than once unsurprisingly) and it's likely you'll have many children – more than three quite possibly.

Pet Power!

And finally . . . pets. They're members of the family too, you know! Check the chart below and discover which animals are for you and which pets you prefer.

Your Sign	Favourite farm animal	Favourite wild animal	Perfect pet	You like a pet to be . . .
Pisces	Sheep	Whale	Goldfish	Dependent
Aries	Ram	Rhino	Rat or mouse	Fast-moving
Taurus	Bull	Elephant	Dog	Reliable
Gemini	Collie dog	Tiger	Parrot	Responsive
Cancer	Pig	Dolphin	Rabbit	Lovable
Leo	Cockerel	Lion	Puppy	Fun
Virgo	Cow	Orang-utan	Budgie	Clean
Libra	Baby chick	Monkey	Cockatoo or dove	Pretty
Scorpio	Goose	Shark	Tarantula or snake	Scary!
Sagittarius	Horse	Zebra	Pony or horse	Sporty
Capricorn	Goat	Crocodile	Cat	Self-sufficient
Aquarius	Donkey	Kangaroo	Tree frog	Interesting

Part 6:
School, Career, Hobbies, Money

Are You The Perfect Pupil?

If you're perfectly honest with yourself, you'd have to admit that school isn't really your "thing". You like seeing your mates and enjoy a couple of subjects (if you're in the right mood), but generally all that getting up early and sitting up straight at a desk is a real pain. You have a fantastic imagination and could do well, but unfortunately this generally positive trait can also hold you back – in that you're always dreamily staring into space and imagining that you're somewhere else.

As a very laid-back person, you have a strong dislike of routines, schedules and timetables and, as most of life at school seems to be based around all these things, you're not likely to feel too comfortable there. In your dream world (where you live half the time!), you'd go to school one day a week and spend the rest of the time having fun.

Most days, you like to keep a low profile and are unlikely to draw attention to yourself by misbehaving or being loud. You're not a natural leader and, in the classroom and the playground, you're happy to follow the lead. You're popular with your classmates, as you always have great ideas for ways of having a laugh, then you're happy to sit back and let others take control. Sadly, because Pisceans are so sweet and easy-going, they're often picked out by bullies and seem to suffer more than the other signs as victims of these intimidating types.

You can just about understand why school is necessary but you really don't see the point of homework and exams. In your eyes, all that extra work is tortuous. Your fave subjects are those that allow you to use your imagination – Art, English (literature and language) and, sometimes, History. You're good at learning and remembering, but only if you're interested in what you're being taught. You're not so hot at memorizing facts, figures and formulae, so may not be top of the class in maths or any of the sciences.

You quite enjoy school trips – mainly because of the break in routine – but would still rather stay at home.

Your worst fault at school is laziness and a general unwillingness to make an effort and this can be very frustrating for your teachers. You're not a rule-breaker by nature, but your negative traits – i.e. your lack of paying attention and your amazing ability to "forget" important instructions – can make you look a bit of a bad girl on occasion. "Could try harder" are words that'll crop up regularly throughout your school life – more often than not, on your annual school reports. But you (and your parents) know what you're like, so that's unlikely to surprise anyone.

If you want to see how your mates compare as schoolmates and pupils, refer to the chart opposite . . .

Study this specially devised chart and work out what kind of student you are . . .

Your Sign	As a student you're . . .	Your fave subject is . . .	Most compatible teacher is . . .	You'd get detention for . . .	Your perfect classmate is . . .
PISCES	Lazy but imaginative	Art	A Taurean	Not paying attention	A Virgoan
ARIES	Noisy but bright	PE	A Geminian	Shouting	A Libran
TAURUS	Slow but determined	Science	A Cancerian	Sulking	A Scorpian
GEMINI	Irritatingly clever	Languages	A Leo	Writing notes	A Sagittarian
CANCER	Quiet and studious	Cookery	A Virgoan	Eating sweets in class	A Capricornian
LEO	Attention-seeking	English language	A Libran	Messing about	An Aquarian
VIRGO	Chatty and hardworking	English literature	A Scorpian	Being cheeky	A Piscean
LIBRA	Lively and creative	Needlework	A Sagittarian	Rule-breaking	An Arien
SCORPIO	Serious and ambitious	History	A Capricornian	Being sarcastic	A Taurean
SAGITTARIUS	Nothing but trouble	Geography	An Aquarian	Not doing your homework	A Geminian
CAPRICORN	Teacher's pet	Maths	A Piscean	Letting your work be copied	A Cancerian
AQUARIUS	A bit hard to handle	Social studies	An Arien	Skiving	A Leo

Just The Job

As with school, you're not happy if your chosen career is too routine or demanding. You're happier as an employee than an employer and need a job where you have a reasonable amount of freedom.

If you're working for a company or organization, you always make the effort to get your work done. Your job needs to be creative in some way – you'll be miserable if you find yourself doing something mundane.

Like many of the other signs, you're affected by your surroundings and won't work well in a drab place. Ideally, you'd like comfort, a relaxed atmosphere, bright colours and lots of space and air.

If you *did* ever end up as a boss, you would be very aware of the needs of your employees.

Because Pisces rules the feet, Pisceans are often found working in a job that involves this part of the body. Shoe design may appeal, as would a job as a reflexologist or chiropodist. As an expressive type, you'd also make a good actor, dancer, designer, painter, poet or writer and, with your psychic ability, may get involved with spiritual work. Some Pisceans end up as priests, nuns, vicars or monks.

Hobbies

Your favourite thing to do, is daydream. You love being at home, where you chill out listening to your favourite music, painting, writing and – of course – fantasizing. You like flowers, small animals and poetry, so having a hobby linked to any of these would be fun for you.

Will You Be Rich?

How likely you are to get rich can depend on your star-sign.

As a Piscean, you're not very moneyminded. You're a bit gullible and are easily "relieved" of your cash (some would say ripped off) by those who are financially more shrewd than you. The strange thing is, that although traditionally you are the least likely sign of the zodiac to become rich, there are plenty of wealthy Pisceans about – though this is more often than not totally accidental!

Astro-cash facts:

- The people most likely to get rich (in this order) are Leos, Taureans, Sagittarians and Virgoans. These signs are closely followed by Aries, Capricorn, Cancer, Scorpio, Libra, Gemini and Aquarius. The least likely sign to accumulate great wealth is Pisces (unless you're Cindy Crawford or Drew Barrymore, that is – both Pisceans and both rather loaded).

- Leos get richest the quickest. But they need to focus on making money and not be distracted by all the other stuff that life hurls their way.

- Cancerians are destined to get rich through their own efforts and shrewdness. They won't get rich, however, if they sit back and relax every time they have a minor success: they must keep on keeping on if they want to make it Branson-style.

- If you were born when Jupiter was in Taurus, great wealth will be yours. Jupiter was in Taurus from 12 April 1964 until 22 April 1965. It moved through the sign again from 26 March 1976 to 22 August 1976 and, again, from 17 October 1976 to 3 April 1977. It returned to Taurus on 9 March 1988 until 21 July 1988, and again from 1 December 1988 until 10 March 1989. Its most recent visit to the sign was on 28 June 1999 where it stayed until 22 October 1999. The next time this transit occurs will be from 15 February 2000 until 29 June 2000. Anyone born during any of these periods is born to be rich!

Part 7:

Holidays

Sun, Sand And Stars!

Pisceans love getting away from the routine of everyday life, so holidays are vital. More than anything, you like peace and quiet, and need to get away more than any of the other signs. If you want to find out which countries are a-calling, how to get there and who your top travelling companion should be, you've come to the right place . . .

As a holidaymaker, like your fellow Water signs, Cancer and Scorpio, you often use holidays as a means of escape. But as a deeply sensitive and emotional person, you need your breaks more than most and should try to make the most of time off. You need peace and quiet and hate being in a hot, crowded place.

Do What? (And Where?)

You love the countryside and holidays in picturesque rented cottages and farmhouses are ideal for you. As a Water sign, you're drawn to the sea, canals, lakes and rivers. Sailing or fishing holidays are perfect. If you're spending summer at home, don't do what everyone else is doing: cycling or picnicking in the country with a friend might be fun, but taking a dip in the local pool (along with the world and its aunt) really won't appeal.

If you decide to spend your summer holidays away from home, you'd choose somewhere quiet and unspoilt. You enjoy peace and relaxation, but are keen to get up and go when the mood takes you – usually at a moment's notice.

How To Get There

If you're going away on holiday, you're not too bothered about how you travel, as you tend to don your Walkman headphones, stick your nose in a book and drift off into a fantasy world until you arrive at your chosen destination. Even so, many Pisceans would prefer not to go anywhere by plane if they had the choice.

Holiday Horrors

Because you live in a bit of a dream world, you always imagine holidays to be one big rose garden and you may be incredibly disappointed when you discover this isn't always the case. If you want to have fun, you can't just sit back and expect it to happen. Don't rely on other people to make you happy: if you want a memorable holiday, you have to go out and make it memorable.

Best Holidays . . .

will be had in Portugal, the Greek islands, Capri and any Scandinavian country.

Holidays
··········

Your Sign	What you need	Holiday love with ...	Activities	Travel ...	Holiday horrors
PISCES	Peace and quiet	a Virgoan	Fishing and picnicking	by boat	Being disappointed
ARIES	Lots of action	a Libran	Pony-trekking and swimming	fast!	Accidents
TAURUS	Time	a Scorpian	Relaxing	slowly	Being too lazy and missing out
GEMINI	Stimulation	a Sagittarian	Socializing and sightseeing	by plane	Stomach upsets
CANCER	Homely surroundings	a Capricornian	All types of watersports	by water	Stress
LEO	Sunshine	an Aquarian	Sunbathing	in style!	Sunburn!
VIRGO	Culture	a Piscean	Skiing and snowboarding	by train	Catching lurgies
LIBRA	New experiences	an Arien	Walking and cycling	first-class	Over-indulgence, in snogging especially!
SCORPIO	Mystery and excitement	a Taurean	Drawing and touring	Taxi!	Dehydration (in hot countries)
SAGITTARIUS	Thrills!	a Geminian	Riding and skateboarding	by motorbike	Being conned
CAPRICORN	Peace and quiet	a Cancerian	Camping	on foot	Getting bored
AQUARIUS	Freedom	a Leo	Safari and nature treks	any way	Running out of money

Part 8:
Party On!

Pisces – The Party Princess!

What's your social style? Are you a party animal or a bit of a party pooper? Read on to find out whether you (and your mates) are the life 'n' soul . . .

You're a laugh-a-minute raver, crazier than most and can bop till you drop! Your attitude to socializing changes all the time though: sometimes you just *have* to go out; other times, you're positively agoraphobic!

Your moods are just as chameleon-like: you can turn an invite down because you're feeling grumpy; then hours (sometimes minutes) later, you'll be feeling just fine and totally regret your rash decision. People never know what to expect when they're out with you, but that's half your appeal. You're rarely antisocial, but you do find it hard to join in if the atmosphere isn't quite right. If you feel comfortable though, you can go totally bonkers. You're generally quite a well-behaved person, so you enjoy letting rip when you get the opportunity. You're not a bad girl, but you sometimes like pretending to be.

Your perfect party: At a club with a few of your best friends.

Craziest party stunt: Being wheeled home in a shopping trolley!

Going out . . . with you can be dangerous!

Staying in . . . is something you need to do more often.

Your Partying Friends

And what about your mates? Here's a quick run-down of the other eleven signs . . .

Aries

Ariens are the absolute life and soul, and the most wanted guests in town! They have the ability to turn a  cosy gathering into a crazy party – they customize the atmosphere to suit themselves. And they couldn't care less what anyone thinks.

Perfect party: An all-night do in a massive club full of thousands of ravers – all close mates, of course!

Craziest party stunt: performing their own version of *Saturday Night Fever* with a mate – in their undies!

Going out . . . is what weekends are for!

Staying in . . . makes them want to go out!

Taurus

Taureans love going out, but they like plenty of warning. Preparing physically, mentally and spiritually for a big night out takes more than a few minutes for a slow-moving Taurean.

Perfect party: A karaoke do in a nice restaurant (Taureans love a good croon), then home to bed – not too late though (Taureans love a good kip too!)

Craziest party stunt: Falling asleep under the pile of coats in the spare room.

Going out . . . is a chore if they're not in the right mood; fine if they are.

Staying in . . . suits their couch-potato personality!

Gemini

All Geminians love their social lives to be varied and thrilling and if they're not, they'll get bored and grumpy. Not that they're asking to be entertained – Gems are more than happy to organize their own activities.

Perfect party: A top house party at a mate's house, where they can arrive early, get ready, and help with the proceedings.

Craziest party stunt: Copping off with every member of the opposite sex there – regardless of who they're going out with! (Tut tut!)

Going out . . . perks 'em up.

Staying in . . . gets 'em down.

Cancer

It has to be said that Cancerians aren't exactly famous for their round-the-clock partying. At the risk of appearing boring, they prefer staying in – especially if there's any eating of delicious snacks to be done!

Perfect party: A dinner party – food cooked by the Cancerian – for a few close chums.

Craziest party stunt: Staying out past midnight.

Going out . . . is unavoidable sometimes.

Staying in . . . means lots of lovely quality time . . . with themselves. Luxury!

Leo

Everyone knows how gorgeous and fun-loving Leos can be, but may *not* know what control freaks they are. Being someone else's guest can be unnerving for a Leo. On the other hand, they make totally fab hosts.

Perfect party: A party at home, with scrummy grub, plenty of dancing and Leo, as ever, in the spotlight.

Craziest party stunt: Going to someone else's party and actually enjoying it!

Going out . . . is fine if they know what to expect and can spend at least *most* of the evening being the centre of attention.

Staying in . . . is a reasonably enjoyable necessity.

Virgo

Virgoans aren't 100 per cent comfortable at a rowdy party. In a Virgoan's view, parties aren't so much social occasions, but are more a way of networking. Most Virgoans prefer spending time in their own company.

Perfect party: A sleep-over with a couple of their closest girl friends.

Craziest party stunt: Dancing.

Going out . . . gives others the pleasure of their marvellous company.

Staying in . . . is boring at worst, blissful at best.

Libra

Librans are the most popular signs of the zodiac and, along with Arians, are Numero Uno party people! Even when they don't really want to go out, it doesn't take much to persuade them.

Perfect party: Librans aren't keen on noise, so a quiet party at a hired room in a restaurant with twenty to thirty friends, some nice music and scrumptious scoff would do just fine.

Craziest party stunt: Dancing on the table, clad in nowt but a feather boa!

Going out . . . is fun but can be tiring.

Staying in . . . is great in the right company.

Scorpio

When it comes to parties, Scorpians like to do the arranging and don't like anyone else interfering. They're good hosts and make polite guests. But however they choose to socialize, they'll always have a good time.

Perfect party: An evening at home. Food may not be a feature, but a Scorpio's guests won't be hungering for fun and games, that's for sure!

Craziest party stunt: Letting out a bottom burp during a game of Twister!! (Oops!)

Going out . . . can be fun – but only if *they've* organized everything.

Staying in . . . means it's time to get to grips with a good book.

Sagittarius

Sagittarians were made for partying. If there's a party on, they don't care where it is – they're there! They have a big reputation for getting even the sleepiest of parties going and are always in hot demand as guests.

Perfect party: Any party – anywhere!

Craziest party stunt: Travelling 500 miles to a party that wasn't actually on. (Oh dear.)

Going out . . . is their reason for living.

Staying in . . . is totally soul-destroying.

Capricorn

Partying is way down a Capricorn's list of priorities. If they *do* go out, they like to decide exactly where they're going, who they're seeing and what they're doing. Someone else's party may be full of too many surprises.

Perfect party: Home alone with a box of popcorn, a pile of magazines and the phone.

Craziest party stunt: Forgetting to bolt the toilet door.

Going out . . . is OK on special occasions.

Staying in . . . is OK any time.

Aquarius

Although they're very sociable, Aquarians aren't really that bothered about partying. They turn down more party invitations than any other sign because, in their view, they've usually got something more interesting to do.

Perfect party: A Green one. (We're talking politics here.)

Craziest party stunt: Riding down the stairs on a trike!

Going out . . . should have a purpose.

Staying in . . . is something they should do more of.

Part 9:

Moon Magic

Moon Rhythms

The moon is the most feminine of the planets, and its waxing and waning affects every female on earth. Check our special chart opposite and discover how it influences you. Then use some moon magic to brighten up your life . . .

Did you know that the human body is approximately 50 per cent water? And that in the same way that the waxing and waning moon pulls the tides of the sea, it can also have a serious pull on our bodies and minds. As the female of the species, we're even more fluid, what with periods and our ability to retain water. Because of this, our health and emotions are closely connected to the phases of the moon. Check the chart opposite and see when the moon's doing what from now till the end of the year 2000 . . .

The Waning Phase

During the **waning phase** (the period between a Full and a New Moon), you'll be at your most serious and probably your quietest. Time should be spent in a meditative way. Many people – females in particular – feel a bit grumpy around this time and are more prone  to sulking than usual. You may find it hard to relax, even though that's exactly what you *should* be doing. Quite often, you'll find that you're very forgetful around this time. If this phase coincides

	WANING	NEW MOON	WAXING	FULL MOON
1999				
Sep/Oct	26th–8th	9th	10th–23rd	24th
Oct/Nov	25th–7th	8th	9th–22nd	23rd
Nov/Dec	24th–6th	7th	8th–21st	22nd
Dec/Jan	23rd–5th	6th	7th–20th	21st
2000				
Jan/Feb	22nd–4th	5th	6th–18th	19th
Feb/Mar	20th–5th	6th	7th–19th	20th
Mar/Apr	21st–3rd	4th	5th–17th	18th
Apr/May	19th–3rd	4th	5th–17th	18th
May/Jun	19th–1st	2nd	3rd–15th	16th
Jun/Jul	17th–30th	1st	2nd–15th	16th
Jul/Aug	17th–30th	31st	1st–14th	15th
Aug/Sep	16th–28th	29th	30th–12th	13th
Sep/Oct	14th–26th	27th	28th–12th	13th
Oct/Nov	14th–26th	27th	28th–10th	11th
Nov/Dec	12th–24th	25th	26th–10th	11th
Dec	12th–24th	25th		

with your pre-period days, everyone had best keep out of your way – you're a total ogre!

When the moon's in its waning phase ...

... spend more time with your family and less with your friends

... rely less on others and more on your own intuition and instincts

. . . operations carried out will be very successful

. . . you're less likely to put on weight (chow down that choc!)

. . . household chores are less of a chore!

What to do

- If you're feeling stressed, do something about it.
- Avoid negative thinking and try to develop a more positive attitude.
- Give yourself some time alone. Take a long bath, listen to some soothing music or have a bit of a cry.
- If you really don't want to be alone, make a date with someone you love and have a good cuddle!

The New Moon

On the day of the **New Moon** (when the moon occupies the same sign as the Sun), you may have new beginnings on your mind. You feel extra energetic and may feel more driven or competitive than usual.

At the time of the New Moon . . .

. . . you're more chatty than usual

. . . your concentration levels are up

. . . people – girls mainly – are in a more optimistic mood

. . . you're keen to get on (procrastinators and slowcoaches will really bug you!)

. . . animals and plants thrive particularly well

. . . your body is especially strong and more resistant than usual to illness

. . . you'll have more success if you make an effort to give up any bad habits you might have

. . . you're more likely to succeed at anything you attempt

What to do

- Don't waste time – there's loads to do, so get on with it!
- Spend time with your girl friends and chat about your needs and desires. (Remember – they'll be affected by the New Moon in much the same way as you are. And you'll have a real psychic connection with mates who share your star sign.)
- Get up early, go for walks, catch up on your letter writing and make phone calls (especially the ones you've been putting off).
- Do some gardening!
- Take up a new hobby or pastime.
- Move house.
- Have another go at something you've previously failed to master. (You're sure to get the hang of it this time.)
- Grab all opportunities.
- Make up with a mate.
- Tune in to your psychic powers!
- Fall in love!

The Waxing Phase

The **waxing**, or first phase, of the moon (the period when the moon appears to grow from what looks like a little piece

of toenail clipping to a big round dinner plate) is generally a very positive time.

When the moon's in its waxing phase ...

... healing of wounds is slower than usual

... you're more likely to put on weight if you're careless about what you eat

... water retention and PMT are more likely to occur

... reactions to toxins are more dramatic

What to do

- Make big decisions.
- Make plans and set yourself goals. This may not be easy but any serious efforts made during these two weeks will almost definitely pay off.

The Full Moon

When the Sun and Moon are in opposite signs of the zodiac and the moon is as round as it can possibly be, it's said to be a **Full Moon**. At this time of the month, regardless of your own personal cycle, you're likely to be more energetic than usual. If you need to tie up any loose ends, do it while the moon is on full beam. In astrology, the Full Moon often indicates the end of a chapter of your life. It can be a sad time, but it's also a time when the old makes way for the new. The Full Moon often indicates that some fab new experiences are coming your way. You should be at your most confident and self-assured and determined enough to succeed in whatever way you want to succeed.

At the time of the Full Moon . . .

. . . you're more likely to sleepwalk

. . . if you cut yourself, you'll bleed more than usual

. . . your period (if you're having one at the time) will be heavier

. . . you're more likely to give birth (if you're pregnant, that is)

What to do

• Surround yourself with bright colours and with people you love.

• Involve yourself in activities that are fun but don't cost too much.

• The Full Moon is a great time for partying! So party!

• Sort out your money problems.

• Expect good news.

• Make some changes at home.

• End that so-called romance (especially if you don't even like the bloke that much).

• Face up to the truth.

Moon Superstitions And Omens

• Never plant anything during the moon's waning phase – it won't grow to its full potential.

• The best time to get a haircut is on the day of the New Moon. Book that appointment now!

• The best marriages start just after a Full Moon.

• A baby born at the Full Moon will grow up to be very

strong. It's also said that if a moon is shining at the time of birth, the baby will be a boy; if there's no moon it'll be a girl. (Never mind genetics, eh?)

- If you steal anything on the third day after a New Moon, you'll most definitely be caught.

- To dream of the Full Moon foretells happiness in love; to dream of the waxing moon means a change for the better; dreaming of the waning moon indicates a change for the worse.

- It's reckoned that the moon can be used to forecast the weather. For example, if the moon is surrounded by a single misty ring, rain's on its way; several circles around the moon predict wet and stormy weather; if the New Moon falls on a Monday (as it did in November 1996 and April and September 1997), it signifies good news and good weather; and if the moon is bright yellow in a cloudless sky, good weather is imminent. Who needs Michael Fish when you've got the Man in the Moon?!

- There are many stories about who the "man in the moon" actually is. The Chinese say he's an old man who binds married couples with silken cord; the Masai of Kenya say he's not a man at all, but a woman with swollen lips and a missing eye – injuries inflicted upon her by her husband, the Sun; and some Germans believe he's an old man who has offended God and is eternally imprisoned on the moon. Quite.

- Turning silver over at the time of a New Moon encourages money to come your way. So check your chart and get flipping!

Part 10:

Your Year Ahead: The Year 2000 At A Glance

The coming twelve months are an action-packed time for Pisceans. With eclipses in January and July; Jupiter changing signs in February and June; and Saturn making transits in August and October, you can expect major happenings galore! For each month of the year, you get a monthly feature, an in-depth week-by-week analysis, as well as an at-a-glance weekly chart to make planning ahead easier. Have a happy year!

JANUARY 2000

New Year, New You!

Stuck for New Year resolution ideas? Then get a load of these . . .

As a crazy **Piscean**, you never know when to stop. In the year 2000, all Pisceans – you included – should make "I think I've gone far enough now, thanks" your own personal slogan. (Get a T-shirt printed if necessary.)

Ariens are impatient little tykes and should stop drumming their fingers on table tops and hopping from foot to foot in bus queues and try to chill out a bit this year.

Taureans are clumsy, stubborn and lazy. So if they want to make some improvements, the question is: where do they start? Any resolution will do really . . .

Geminians are always flitting around, calling people they don't like in the slightest "daaarling" and kissing the air. So, really, their New Year's resolution should be to stop being so superficial. NOW!

Cancerians never stop droning on about their terrible lot in life. So the best New Year resolution for a moany old crab? To stop blubbing over nothing and being such an old drama queen!

Leos are too bossy for their own pants. If they're going to make a New Year resolution, they should remember not to treat other people like servants. (Unless they ask very nicely, of course . . .)

Virgoans love pick, pick, picking holes. If they're not careful, everything around them will soon look rather colander-like. Their New Year resolution should be to at least *try* saying nice things to people occasionally.

Librans are lazy lunks and should resolve to get up out of the midden they live in and have a darn good spring-clean. And they should have a bath while they're at it!

Scorpians should make an effort to be more trusting. They're so paranoid they think everyone's out to get them. Their New Year's resolution? To start believing that a lot of people really *do* have faith in them.

Sagittarians have enormous big mouths, which they are forever putting their huge size 12s in! The Saggie resolution for the coming year should be to be less "honest" – and to get their feet surgically trimmed. (Only joking . . . about the feet, that is!)

Capricornians secretly love putting a damper on other people's high spirits. They also love saying "no" for the sake of it. Their New Year's resolution for the year 2000 must be to say "yes, please" instead of "oooh, not for me thanks – I'm trying to give up" once in a while.

Key to Symbols

LOVE:

 Snog overload

 Kiss him with caution

 Not a lotta totty

FRIENDS:

 Little Miss Popular

 All's fine and dandy

 Watch what you say

SOCIAL LIFE:

 Prepare to partee!

 Stay cool – don't overdo it

 Time to stay in 'n' chill

Aquarians like being cool, but sometimes they go below freezing point. They should try being more cuddly and affectionate this year.

JANUARY FORECAST

1st—7th

Mars enters Pisces, making you feel energetic but agitated with it. Put your energy into something constructive; bottling it up won't do you any good at all, and it could express itself through accident or illness, especially if you've been feeling a bit fragile lately.

Love: *Friends:* 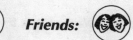   *Social life:*

8th—14th

This week, the planet of responsibility, Saturn, changes direction in the communications part of your chart, which could cause a minor bout of depression. Not good. Make an effort to see your friends: holing yourself up in your room won't help. And try to be less negative: it's almost as if you're bringing all this bad stuff on yourself.

Love: *Friends:* 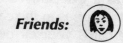   *Social life:*

15th—21st

Mercury's position this week means you refuse to believe anything unless you hear it straight from the horse's mouth. Gossip is of no interest to you: there are

See page 176 for key to symbols

far more important things to think about right now – like yourself!

Love: **Friends:**   **Social life:**

22nd–31st

In the wake of the eclipse in your opposite sign on the 21st, you could experience problems either at school or with your health. But don't worry – these will right themselves fairly quickly . . .

Love: **Friends:**   **Social life:**

FEBRUARY 2000

Funny Valentines

Did you know that your star sign determines the sort of Valentine you'd make? Look up your sign and check whether you'll be giving or receiving (or both) this February 14th.

Everyone knows that, as a **Piscean**, you're a real old sop: you not only pen the verses in the cards you send, but you also *make* the cards yourself out of a pair of your old frilly pants. Then you write a song, record it on a cassette, Sellotape it inside the card and send the whole shiboodle to your "cherie amour". (Pass the sick bucket please . . .) You're also the type of person who sends cards to her mum and to the ugly girl in class.

See page 176 for key to symbols

Ariens are sexy but not particularly romantic. They prefer saucy underwear to a 'ickle teddy bear with "I Wuv Oo" embroidered on its furry tum. If they actually *remember* V. Day, they'll probably forget the card, flowers and chocs and buy their loved one something small and frothy instead (and we're not talking milkshakes here).

Taureans are extremely romantic and very sensual. Not only will they be buying their Valentine flowers and jewels, but they'll probably stretch to a jar of chocolate body paint too. Mmmm . . . delish!

Geminians think V. Day is v. exciting, but only if they get tons of cards from secret admirers. The thing is though – they're so busy thinking about themselves, they clean forget to buy anything for their paramours. (Oops!)

Cancerians are extremely romantic and will be arranging all sorts of lovely slushy surprises for their darling. A candlelit dinner, a stroll in the moonlight and snogs a-plenty – that's what they'll be giving their sweetheart on V. Day.

Leos are madly extravagant and love to splash out on their loved ones. The trouble is that they do need a bit of a nudge sometimes. If a lovestruck someone dropped them a line (or a hint) prior to the big day, they'd be only too happy to oblige with love gifts a-plenty. Otherwise, they might not bother . . .

Virgoans are a bit stingy, so if the person they love is waiting by their letterbox for flowers, choccies and heart-shaped cushions with balloons attached with loads of love from a Virgoan paramour, they could be waiting a very long time indeed!

Librans are just about the silliest, slushiest, most romantic sign of the zodiac. If a lissome and lovely Libran was to be your Valentine, they'd go the whole hog, don a frilly apron and be your love slave for the day, whether that's what you wanted or not . . .

Scorpians love all the mystery, intrigue and question marks that surround Valentine's Day. But because they don't have a deep need to be appreciated (they actually get quite embarrassed when people get all grateful), anyone who receives a card from a Scorpian will never, ever know who it's from . . .

Sagittarians don't expect to get any cards and only send them if they're under immense pressure. They're notoriously lazy and unreliable too. If someone paid them a lot of money, maybe they'd send one. But then again, maybe they still wouldn't bother.

Capricornians will always send V. Day gifts (on the right day too!), but they don't like to buy anything too expensive, too tacky or too imaginative. Looks like a nice box of chocs is the order of the day then . . .

Aquarians like to throw Valentine's Day parties, then pretend they forgot it was Valentine's Day, then get loads of cards and love gifts from all their guests and not give out any themselves. Very clever . . .

FEBRUARY FORECAST

1st–7th

Mercury in your sign makes you kinda fidgety and restless. You need to keep busy or you'll go crazy. You're very expressive this week and, using your powers of speaking and writing, you should be able to get pretty much anything you want – within reason of course! The New Moon on the 5th indicates romance: in fact, you could be completely bowled over by a gorgeous guy at an early Valentine's Day party. Very nice . . .

Love: *Friends:*   *Social life:*

8th–14th

You start the week with the Moon in your sign which makes you rather sensitive – not so much to other people's feelings, just to your own. Avoid heavy discussions this week – you just won't be able to see things from someone else's point of view.

Love: *Friends:*  *Social life:*

15th–21st

As the Sun has now moved into your sign you're in a happy-go-lucky, confident and enthusiastic mood. You're full of energy and are ready for anything. If a problem needs to be solved though, don't try to do it now: there are too many other fun things to do instead. With Venus in your sign this week, you're in a hyper-sociable mood. Spend as much time as you can with

See page 176 for key to symbols

people you love, but try not to neglect your school work. People are queueing up to be your mate and you're the first name on everybody's party list.

Love: *Friends:* 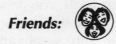 *Social life:*

22nd–29th

Jupiter has changed signs and is now in the process of settling into your astrological house of communications. This means that if you're feeling bored with the sheer tedium of your life, now's the time to do something about it. Taking on a new hobby or trying out a new subject at school could help. Money matters are well starred this week too and a close friend or relative could get lucky – something which will ultimately benefit you as much as them.

Love: *Friends:*   *Social life:*

MARCH 2000

Don't Forget Mother's Day!

March is for mums – so don't forget to buy her something gorgeous on M. Day itself. If you're stuck for ideas, consider these . . .

Arien mums aren't as frumpy as they sometimes look and would be quite distressed if you bought them a nice oven glove or apron for Mother's Day. Buy them the latest Verve CD though and they'd be well flattered.

Taurean mums are very practical and like gardening, so a nice trowel would be the ideal Mother's Day gift. They're also partial to a bit of chocolate, so a *chocolate* trowel would be even better.

Geminian mums like surprises and would hate anything as clichéd as flowers or chocolates. They love a good read – nothing too heavy, mind – and would really appreciate an annual subscription to a posh magazine.

Cancerian mums are real home lovers, so anything for the house would be a good gift. Food goes down a treat – especially the gourmet variety – as does a nice leafy plant. Easy to please or what?

Leo mums aren't too bothered about what pressie you actually buy them: as long as it's BIG, they'll be totally impressed by it. They also like anything glittery, shiny or sparkly – never mind the quality, it's the size and the UV factor that matters.

Virgoan mums just *love* tidying up. They like their bodies, homes and cars to be sweet-smelling and clean at all times. If your ma's a Virgo, buy her a nice bar of soap, a mini-vac or a Magic Tree air freshener for the car.

Libran mums adore being fussed over and love receiving cards (home-made ones are their faves). On Mother's Day, tell her she looks gorgeous and that you love her, then present her with your latest artistic masterpiece. She'll be completely chuffed.

Scorpian mums like curling up on the sofa with a good book. For Mother's Day, find out her favourite author and buy her a copy of his/her most recent novel. (Make sure she hasn't got it already though. Scorpio mums have a sneaky habit of buying books on the quiet.)

Sagittarian mums really aren't fussy about what presents they get. As far as they're concerned, it's the thought that counts. If you remember Mother's Day at all, they'll be over the moon. And if you can't stretch to a costly gift, a big kiss and a "love you, Mum" will do just fine.

Capricornian mums, it has to be said, are slightly martyrish. They'll say (well in advance of Mother's Day) "No, really, Mother's Day – pah! I don't believe in it – I'd be much happier if you didn't get me anything . . . " but then they get really upset when you do as you're told. So ignore what she says. Make a big fuss of her. Make her a cake. Buy her flowers. It'll make your life a lot easier all round.

Aquarian mums are pretty charitable types. If you told her you weren't going to buy her a Mother's Day present, but that you were going to donate some money to her favourite charity instead, she'd be well impressed. But secretly she'd be equally thrilled with a comedy video, CD or diary.

Piscean mums are dreamy and romantic, and really look forward to Mother's Day. Make it worth waiting for by presenting her with a book of romantic poetry, a bottle of champagne or a big bunch of lilies. Whatever you buy, make sure it's wrapped nicely – Pisceans love a bit of fancy wrapping.

MARCH FORECAST

<u>1st–7th</u>

The New Moon in your sign means a brand new start. Many Pisceans will be changing their image this week. If you're one of them, you've picked the right time to do it.

Love: *Friends:*  *Social life:*

<u>8th–14th</u>

Venus enters Pisces, making you feel mega-relaxed. You're in a pleasant and sociable mood. If you've any obligations to fulfil (i.e. visiting dull relatives you haven't seen for yonks), do it this week. You're so charming and sociable, they won't even notice how bored you are in their company!

Love: *Friends:*  *Social life:*

<u>15th–21st</u>

With gorgeous planet Venus in your sign all week, you're feeling utterly fab. Getting your money problems sorted helps of course, but you'd be feeling confident even without this influence. Bit lacking on the boy front, but you're having so much fun you're not overly bothered . . . You're the girl everyone wants to hang out with and you're looking babelicious too! What an excellent week!

See page 176 for key to symbols

Love: **Friends:**  **Social life:**

22nd–31st

Mars in the communciations part of your chart from the 23rd sees you making some positive moves to change your life. You know what's got to be done. So go ahead and do it. Then don't look back . . .

Love: **Friends:** 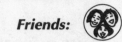 **Social life:**

APRIL 2000

Are You An Easter Chick?

The Easter hols are here, which means lots of choc and no school. Great! Not so great though is the constant round of visiting relatives and night after night of tedious TV. Read on to discover whether Easter is your "thing" . . .

As a **Piscean**, you really enjoy and appreciate your privacy, so the thought of a whole barrage of relatives coming over for Easter Sunday lunch sends shivers up your sensitive little spine. Ideally, you'd spend the hols lolling around in a negligee, daintily munching on a few Milk Tray, and saying "I want to be alone" to anyone who dares to crowd your space. And why not indeed?!

See page 176 for key to symbols

Ariens love the holidays, but can't abide Easter itself. It's the crap telly that upsets them the most. All those variety performances! Breaking up from school is fab – there's no denying that. But it's all downhill after that really.

Taureans' favourite part of the Easter break is all the lovely chocolate! They're determined to eat as many Easter eggs as is humanly possible and then spend the rest of the hols feeling bilious. Mmm . . . fun . . .

Geminians like the excitement surrounding Easter but, unless they're religious types, can't really understand what all the fuss is about. If the Easter Bunny was real though . . . now that'd be a different matter altogether.

Cancerians love a nice family get-together, so if there are any rellos visiting or to be visited, Cancer will be in their element. The best bit about Easter, as far as they're concerned, is all the home-made cakes (especially the hot cross buns). Yum!

Leos see Easter as an opportunity to buy their nearest and dearest some lovely choccy gifts. It's a little-known astrological fact that most people who shop at Thornton's over the Easter period are Leos. (Maybe.)

Virgoans think Easter is a silly and frivolous waste of time. In their opinion, it's a waste of valuable school time and if they had their way, there wouldn't be any Easter holidays at all. (The summer hols would be extended by two weeks instead.)

Librans like everything to do with Easter – the cards, the Easter eggs, the "Jesus" films on TV and the family gatherings. Why it's just like Christmas, but with daffodils and bunnies and little fluffy yellow chicks. (OK, that's enough, Libra!)

Scorpians really like the fact that everything goes a bit quiet over Easter and that they can relax for a short moment in their otherwise hectic lives. Trouble is, year after year, they always invite tons of relatives round for celebratory drinks and snacks, thus making Easter more hard work than any other time of year. And they never learn either . . .

Sagittarians, unless deeply religious, couldn't give a monkey's about Easter. They're more than likely to use the time off to go somewhere as far away from home as possible (somewhere they don't celebrate Easter preferably . . .).

Capricornians don't particularly like Easter but feel it's their duty to celebrate it. This means doing all the traditional stuff associated with the festival, such as baking hot cross buns, giving (and scoffing) Easter eggs, and having people round for tea. Then moaning about it. A lot.

Aquarians like having time off from school, but aren't overly bothered about celebrating Easter in the traditional way. No, they're more likely to use the hols as a time to catch up on the soaps, read a couple of books and update their diary.

APRIL FORECAST

1st–7th
The New Moon and the Sun in the money part of your chart marks the start of a prosperous phase. It's a good time to make money, open a savings account or get your finances sorted.

Love: *Friends:*   *Social life:*

8th–14th
As Mercury leaves your sign, you become more settled. Keep an eye on your money though and don't lend or give a penny to anyone, no matter how convincing a sob story they give you.

Love: *Friends:*   *Social life:*

15th–21st
As the Sun changes signs, you're full of enthusiasm and confidence and can communicate with others on every level. You're at your most persuasive too – so if you want something, now's the time to ask.

Love: *Friends:*    *Social life:*

22nd–30th
The last week of April is destined to be a very quiet one for you, which is probably for the best. So much has been going on in your life lately, you could do with a rest. So take one while you can . . .

See page 176 for key to symbols

Love: **Friends:** **Social life:**

MAY 2000

Spring Fever!

At this time of the year, all the signs of the zodiac tend to get a tad frisky. Some more than others . . .

As a slush-puppy **Piscean**, you would spend the whole of spring in Paris if you could – it's just *sooo* romantic there (so you've heard). If you haven't a paramour at this time of year, you'll spend every waking hour searching for one. Spring fever at its worst . . .

Ariens are seriously affected by the warmer weather and can go a bit crazy if not carefully monitored. Arian females can't get enough of the boys at this time of year and seem to fancy every single one they see. Careful now . . .

Taureans feel the effects of the spring – there's no denying that. But the only action they're likely to take is to swap their 13-tog duvet for a 10-tog one, then to snuggle back down . . .

Geminians go ever so slightly bonkers when the spring kicks in. All they want to do is go out and have a good time. (So what's new then?)

Cancerians are seriously affected by the spring, in that all they can think about is redecorating. Come May,

See page 176 for key to symbols

there's a huge increase in the number of folk hanging out at B&Q, and, guess what – most of them are Cancerians. Allegedly.

Leos, at the first sign of warm weather, start stripping off and baring their bods to the sunshine. They don't actually care if the rest of the world is still wearing its anorak – a string vest and Bermuda shorts will do Leo just fine.

Virgoans go mad in the spring all right. All they want to do is spring-clean. "That spring sunshine doesn't half show up the dust", you'll hear them say at least twelve times a day, as they gad about brandishing a feather duster.

Librans find this time of year the most romantic time of all. If they don't go actively looking for love in May, then they'll hole themselves up at home with a big stack of weepy black-and-white movies and a pile of lace hankies, and get soppy on their own instead.

Scorpians are a sexy bunch, and start to feel their sap rising at the mere mention of spring. Almost all of the opposite sex become irresistibly attractive to Scorpians at this time of year and many of them start a passionate romance in May. Come summer though, they realize what a mistake they've made. (Oops!)

Sagittarians get itchy feet (and we're not talking athlete's foot here) in the spring and can't wait to get away. Many of them *have* to wait though, so at this time of year their craziness isn't due so much to spring fever, as to the fact that they can't do as they want.

Capricornians are *never* crazy: they're just too sensible to let anything – spring included – make them behave out of character. They might – just *might* – turn up the volume on their transistor radio a smidgen, but that's about as far as it goes.

Aquarians are pretty crazy at the best of times, so the time of year doesn't really make much difference. Spring sometimes brings out their creative side though, and many an Aquarian will be seen sporting a beret and brandishing a paintbrush in May.

MAY FORECAST

1st–7th

Mercury in the communications part of your chart provides you with brilliant insight and great wit. If you need to impress anyone, you'll do it ten times over this week. In fact, you even impress *yourself* with your eloquence and charm! Mars in the domestic part of your chart from the 4th indicates rows galore at home. A certain male personage is annoying you big time and seems intent on making life hard for you. But maybe your attitude is winding him up. Think about it and see what you can do to make amends.

Love: *Friends:*   *Social life:*

8th–14th

If you're taking any tests or exams this week, you'll do especially well. Entering competitions is well starred too, so give that a try if you can squeeze it in between all the school work!

See page 176 for key to symbols

Love: Friends:    Social life:

15th—21st

The Full Moon in the travel part of your chart indicates some connections with distant countries. You may be taking an early summer holiday – or at the very least *planning* a trip away.

Love: Friends:    Social life:

22nd—31st

The Sun and Mercury in the home and family section of your chart mean all problems are finally resolved with close relatives (namely parents and/or siblings). In fact, being with your family is your top pastime this week. (Which is lucky, because now it's the half-term hols you may not have much choice *but* to be with them.) You're at your most eloquent too, so use your gift of the gab, not only to get your own way, but to charm your way back into their hearts.

Love: Friends: Social life:

JUNE 2000

... And Don't Forget Father's Day Either!

If you want to buy your Dad a special gift on Father's Day, why bother when

he'd much rather you did something else? Want to know more? Then keep reading . . .

Arien dads quite like the idea of Father's Day. In fact, they like the idea of anything that means they're the focus of everyone's attention. If your Pop's an Arian, he's no exception. He's not bothered about pressies though – he'd much rather you challenged him to a game of footie down the park.

Taurean dads find all that Father's Day malarkey a bit embarrassing and would prefer it if you just let him have an extra long lie-in – all day preferably – then brought him the papers and a nice cup of tea. (Aw, he doesn't ask for much, does he?)

Geminian dads aren't usually around much, but they'd really appreciate a phone call (wherever they might be). Cheap if he's in Bognor – a tidy sum if he's in Bangladesh!

Cancerian dads love photos, so take him down to the photo booth at Woolies, get a strip of funny "instant" pics of you and him pulling funny faces, and stick 'em in a photo album. A lovely and unusual gift that costs not very much.

Leo dads like their kids to appreciate them. Usually they like really big, expensive presents, but if you could spend the whole of Father's Day telling him what a top bloke he is and how he's the best dad in the cosmiverse, you could save yourself a whole load of cash.

Virgoan dads enjoy intellectual pursuits, so on Father's Day, instead of buying him a mug with "The World's No. 1 Dad" emblazoned on it, pretend you're Magnus Magnusson and invite him to appear on your own special edition of *Mastermind*. (He'll think he's in heaven!)

Libran dads love people doing things for them. On Father's Day, ask him if there's anything he wants doing and he's sure to present you with a big, long list. After cleaning the car, polishing his shoes (all of them) and filing all his bills, you'll be fed up, but he'll have had a nice time.

Scorpian dads love winning so, on Father's Day, challenge him to a game of Scrabble or three and let him win. He'll be *sooo* happy!

Sagittarian dads love a pint. So take him down the pub and give him a couple of quid to buy himself one. (If you're under age and not allowed in, you can sit outside in the car with a bag of crisps and a bottle of pop till he's finished.)

Capricornian dads really enjoy curries. They're a bit expensive from the local takeaway mind, so why not attempt to make your own from ingredients already in your kitchen cupboard? Look to your mum's Madhur Jaffrey cookbook for inspiration . . .

Aquarian dads really like dancing. The only problem is, they're not very good at it and usually end up looking like right plonkers! On Father's Day, allow him to dance to his heart's content – and *don't* laugh (not even a little bit).

Piscean dads' preferred pastime is watching videos. On Father's Day, hire a few of his all-time fave movies and let him watch them till his eyes go square. Then return the vids to the hire shop for him: that's the bit he hates most.

JUNE FORECAST

1st–7th

Venus in the domestic part of your chart bodes well for family get-togethers. If a relative is celebrating this week, you'll have fun celebrating with them. Anything to do with weddings or engagements is especially well starred.

Love: *Friends:*   *Social life:*

8th–14th

Mercury, in the romance part of your chart all week long, indicates that love and fun are coming your way by the bucketload! People younger than you feature in your life at the moment, and could bring you luck. So don't turn down any baby-sitting jobs this week, will you?

See page 176 for key to symbols

Love: **Friends:** 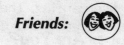   **Social life:**

15th–21st

The Full Moon in the ambitions part of your chart indicates big changes at school. You may feel unhappy about this at first, but the planets advise you not to complain too much and just go with the flow. You'll realize why all that's happening now is a good thing in a few weeks' time. Mars changes signs on the 17th and you're hot, hot, hot! Love is coming at ya, and you can't get enough of the opposite sex! If you want someone, go get 'em! They're putty in your hands.

Love: **Friends:**   **Social life:**

22nd–30th

With Venus, Mercury and Mars in your astrological house of fun and frolics, you're in the mood for love. Work is a definite no-no, so anything connected with school is quite painful – especially if there's some unfinished business to be dealt with. If there is, don't leave it any longer: deal with it now – it could be your last chance. When the Sun joins the other planets, if you're looking for romance, you could well find it in the form of someone you see every day. If you're looking for comic moments, see your mates: they're sure to have you in stitches this week.

Love: **Friends:**   **Social life:**

See page 176 for key to symbols

JULY 2000

What Sort Of Shopper Are You?

Now the summer sales are on, will you be dashing out spending? Much of your shopping style depends on your star sign. For example . . .

As a **Piscean**, you're a bit of a day dreamer. You tend to get a very vague idea of what it is you want to buy, then spend most of your life looking for it. Chances are, your dream purchase doesn't actually exist! But because you love browsing, you don't really care.

Arien shoppers are incredibly impatient. They won't be found waiting in a long queue to pay for *anything* – not even the world's best bargain. They're naturally impulsive too, which means they've got a wardrobe-full of purchases that never should have been.

Taureans like to take their time when they go on a spree, and enjoy making a day of it – starting early, stopping for a snack, then continuing to browse. When they find something they like, they splash out. Otherwise, that purse remains tightly shut.

Geminians can spend a record amount of cash in a very limited time but sometimes lose their sense of judgment in the process. They love shopping and usually return with armloads of stuff – most of which will stay in the carrier bags for ever more!

Cancerian folk are careful shoppers and won't buy unless they're sure they really *will* use their purchase.

They don't mind spending a lot – as long as it's on themselves. Buying presents for others is *not* their speciality by any stretch of the imagination.

Leo shoppers are wildly extravagant – always ready to treat themselves and others – and will always spend far more than they mean to. In fact, if someone goes out for a packet of Rolos and comes back with half of Miss Selfridge, chances are they're a Leo.

Virgoans are extremely fussy and, when shopping, will to and fro between shops for hours. Unless the potential purchase is perfect in every way and has a myriad of uses, they won't buy it. Fact: Virgoans are the shoppers most likely to return home empty-handed.

Librans like shopping and can be extravagant when the mood takes them. They're real ditherers, though, and because they find it hard to make up their minds, they often buy everything in sight (just in case) and end up very confused – not to mention broke.

Scorpians – males and females alike – have a reputation for being careful with their cash but they secretly love to spend, saving their money, then blowing it all in a single day! Big purchases appeal most – the more expensive, the better.

Sagittarians shop in a most haphazard fashion, and can spend hours running about, not knowing what they want or what to buy. They buy a lot of things that they think will come in handy, but most of the stuff they come home with is, in fact, pretty useless.

Capricornians are the most cautious shoppers of all

and don't really like to part with their hard-earned dosh, preferring instead to save it all up. Purchases are made only when necessary, and the word "spree" doesn't actually feature in their vocabulary. And, although prudent, they're the most likely sign to avoid the sales.

Aquarians can be a tad antisocial and would rather do their shopping by mail order than fighting the high street crowds. Computer-literate Aquarians surf the Internet and shop that way – then get the goods delivered to their door. More civilized by far!

JULY FORECAST

1st–7th
The New Moon in the romance part of your chart means a romance is on the cards. If you're boy-free, you could well meet someone really cute this week. If you're seeing someone, you may just fall in love.

Love: **Friends:**  **Social life:**

8th–14th
After Jupiter's most recent transit into the domestic part of your chart on June 30th, you may be thinking about changing your immediate surroundings. Many Pisceans will be swapping rooms with a sibling, doing a spot of redecorating or actually moving house. Whichever – it's a good way to go and should cheer you up no end.

Love: **Friends:** 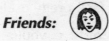 **Social life:**

See page 176 for key to symbols

15th–21st

This week's eclipse suggests it's high time you took a close look at some of your so-called "mates". Some of them haven't really got your interests at heart and are only hanging out with you for selfish reasons. One friendship may have to end, but this just leaves a gap which will soon be filled by someone new – and less selfish.

Love: *Friends:*   *Social life:*

22nd–31st

The New Moon and the Sun in the health part of your chart on the 31st suggests that you stop taking on so much – let others take the strain sometimes. School's well starred at the moment, as long as you make sure you don't give in to laziness. Get set for some hard graft . . .

Love: *Friends:* 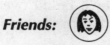 *Social life:*

AUGUST 2000

Holiday Romance

To some people, the summer is all about love. Are you the sort to indulge in a holiday romance? It all depends on your star sign . . .

As a **Piscean**, and whether you're

See page 176 for key to symbols

attached or single, you are always in demand when on holiday. You're very romantic and love the idea of a holiday romance, but the passionate affair you envisage often turns out to be no more than a rather depressing one-night (or two-week) stand. If you take your boyfriend on holiday, your "grass is always greener" attitude could cause a row or two.

Ariens love an adventure of the romantic variety and what better way to indulge than to have a holiday romance? If they go on holiday with a boyfriend, the whole thing will be a bit of a snogsome affair. If they go without a bloke, their holiday becomes one great flirtathlon!

Taureans want a good time and if a romance happens whilst on holiday, it's a bonus. They don't go out of their way to find a bloke, but they'll certainly indulge in a fair bit of flirting. If they take a boyfriend on holiday with them, they'll be all over each other; if they go away single, they're likely to come back in love.

Geminians are the biggest flirts of the zodiac. Holiday romances were made for them. The thing they like most about summer flings is their brevity and the fact that they don't have to see the bloke ever again! Few Gemini girls take a boyfriend away with them but, with or without a boyfriend in tow, Miss Gemini will have a whale of a time.

Cancerians often fantasize about meeting a handsome foreigner and falling in love and, because of that, holiday romance is a serious business for them. They're destined to have several romances abroad. They're convinced they're the "real thing" and are disappointed when they discover they're not. If they holiday with a boyfriend, they'll only have eyes for him; if they go in search of love, they'll find it in one form or another.

Leos, when they get involved with someone on holiday, enjoy the snogging but rarely fall in love. If they go away with a boyfriend, they'll spend half their time eating, the other half snogging. If they go blokeless, they make sure they have fun – and that includes dancing the night away, attempting to pull every half-decent bloke in sight!

Virgoans don't really like foreign affairs, but that doesn't mean they completely rule out the chance of holiday romance. They're not into casual relationships or one-night stands, and as many holiday love scenarios *are* casual, Virgoans go out of their way not to get involved. Holidaying with a boyfriend is more their thing; and they'd rather stay at home than go on holiday alone.

Librans love the idea of a holiday romance. A romance abroad is a romance made in heaven as far as they're concerned. Flirtatious by nature, they love the thrill of the chase and when they go on holiday, they don't stop running for a second! They tend to get involved very quickly though, and this can lead to many regrets.

Scorpians are sexy enough to know they can have a

holiday romance if they want one, but chances are they're just not interested. They like to have a good time when they're on holiday, and having an affair just detracts from this in their opinion. They take love seriously and won't have a fling just for the fun of it. They like to holiday alone and won't stand for being pestered by any local romeos.

Sagittarians see holiday romances as just one of their many hobbies! If they see someone they fancy on holiday (and they usually do – on the first day more often than not!), they get to work quickly. Language differences pose no problems for them – they're quite adept at interpreting body language!

Capricornians go on holiday to see the sights, sample the culture and have a good time. Having a holiday fling doesn't really come into it. They're cautious by nature and believe that brief holiday encounters are quite risky. That's why they avoid them like the plague.

Aquarians don't often holiday in very romantic places, but if they happen to come across a bloke who shares their interests and beliefs, they won't mind seeing him once or twice during the holiday. Aquarians in a relationship may need to holiday alone; it's not just school they need a break from!

AUGUST FORECAST

1st–7th
Mars in your astrological house of health advises you to really look after yourself. Many Pisceans will suffer headaches under this transit. So take it easy if you can.

Love: **Friends:**    **Social life:**

8th–14th

Mercury joining Mars in your astrological house of health could mean a minor malady. You're a bit stressed out and should stop taking on so much. OK, so there's a lot to do, but maybe it's time to let someone else take the strain – for a few days anyway.

Love: **Friends:** 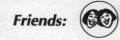   **Social life:**

15th–21st

Saturn is now settled in your astrological house of home and family, and this could be making you feel a tad paranoid – about certain relatives in particular. You think a parent or sibling has it in for you, but could you be imagining it? Something which happened in the past could come back to haunt you (as it has done before), and you're not happy about this. Do all you can to exorcize these "ghosts". Do it by talking to older relatives and finding out the truth.

Love: **Friends:**    **Social life:**

22nd–31st

With three planets – the Sun, Venus and Mercury – in your opposite sign, romance is extremely well starred. If you're dating someone, this could be love. If you're single, you won't be for much longer. Brace yourself . . . Thanks to the New Moon on the 29th, you can expect passion galore. If you're away from home

See page 176 for key to symbols

this week, this could indicate the start of a sizzlingly hot holiday romance. If you're tempted into being unfaithful (i.e. if you already have a boyfriend at home), tread carefully. Maybe it'd be better to hang on to him and give this holiday Romeo a miss. Think about it . . .

Love: *Friends:*   *Social life:*

SEPTEMBER 2000

Star Students

September means one thing: no more summer holidays. School – depending on your star sign – brings either great sadness or great joy. Find out how you'll be feeling as the new term begins . . .

As a creative and imaginative **Piscean**, you love doodling and writing poetry. But that's about it. School you do not love at all. Ask you to do anything involving numbers, chemicals or common sense and you blow a fuse. (Most frequently heard refrain from Teach: "Recite the chemical symbol for potassium chloride and tuck those wires back in your ears!")

Ariens are excellent at PE. If "attention-seeking" was a subject, they'd be great at that too. If they didn't enjoy sitting in the back row of the class so much, they'd be grade A students. (Most frequently heard refrain from Teach: "Come and sit at the front right NOW!")

Taureans progress slowly but surely with most subjects,

See page 176 for key to symbols

but if they want to excel they'll have to stop being so stubborn. Unless they pay more attention, they're destined to be dunces. (Most frequently heard refrain from Teach: "Go and stand in the corner and don the pointy hat!")

Geminians are irritatingly intelligent and, although they're not particularly brilliant at any one subject, they do OK. They *will* insist on getting up to mischief in class though. (Most frequently heard refrain from Teach: "Is it something you'd like to share with the rest of the class?")

Cancerians are quite good students but really need to swot to get good grades. They have to be in the right mood to concentrate though (when it's a New Moon preferably), and spend many a lesson staring blankly out of the window. (Most frequently heard refrain from Teach: "What *is* it that's so interesting out there?")

Leos love messing about. To a Leo, lessons are annoying interruptions to the one long lunch break that is their life. If they could be bothered to come in from the playground, they'd probably do quite well. (Most frequently heard refrain from Teach: "Didn't you hear the bell, cloth-ears?")

Virgoans insist on doing everything in their own inimitable style. They're popular with classmates, but teachers can't abide their Norman Know-it-all ways. (Most frequently heard refrain from Teach: "Put your hand down and let someone else answer!")

Librans think school is a right laugh. It's where they conduct their social life. They're not so keen on the lessons though. The teachers spoil things a bit too. And as for rules – well they're fun to break, but that's all. (Most frequently heard refrain from Teach: "Could you *please* turn off that mobile phone?!")

Scorpians are swots. With their photographic memories, they just love remembering great long lists of dates and formulae. And as for exams – why, they're a complete doddle! (Most frequently heard refrain from Teach: "Take this certificate of merit and go to the top of the class!")

Sagittarians detest school. They're the naughtiest people in the class and can be extremely disruptive. They drive even the most tolerant teacher to distraction because they never, *ever* do as they're told. (Most frequently heard refrain from Teach: "What's your excuse *this* time?")

Capricornians are the teachers' pets of the zodiac. They're quiet and studious, yet strangely not very bright. Despite this, all their mates copy from them. (Most frequently heard refrain from Teach: "Why has everyone else in the class got the same (wrong) answers as you?")

Aquarians like doing everything their own way and that doesn't go down too well with the teachers. They also love skiving. In fact, given the choice, they wouldn't bother with school at all. (Most frequently heard refrain from Teach: "Where were you yesterday during double biology?")

SEPTEMBER FORECAST

1st–7th

You're at your most sexy as the new school term begins, thanks to the most recent Venus transit on August 31st. You're a big hit with everyone you meet – especially the blokes! – and can use your sex appeal to get your own way in every situation. Mercury has changed signs and surrounds you with secrets this week. Luckily, you're good at keeping schtum (which is very frustrating for close mates who are desperate for gossip – especially that Gemini friend of yours!). No matter how much you're tempted to blab, keep quiet – you'll get into big trouble otherwise.

Love: **Friends:** 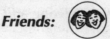 **Social life:**

8th–14th

As Saturn starts moving backwards this week, life at home takes on a serious air. If someone's been nagging you to take on extra responsibility, there could be problems. Maybe you're just not ready for that yet . . .

Love: **Friends:**  **Social life:**

15th–21st

Mars in your opposite sign means you can expect rows a-plenty between you and someone you're close to. This could be a boyfriend or your best mate – whoever, it'll be a painful experience. The only way to make amends is to back down and admit you were in the wrong. (Even if you weren't.) It's the only way.

See page 176 for key to symbols

Love: **Friends:**   **Social life:**

22nd–30th

Venus in the travel part of your chart forecasts time away from home. Many Pisceans will be spending the weekend away from home; others will be expanding their horizons in other ways. Whatever you do, you're likely to end up a whole lot wiser for it. The New Moon in the passion part of your chart on the 27th signifies the occurrence of a major chemistry thing with a sexy guy. If you're single, this is great news, but if you're already seeing someone, this meeting could cause complications. Bear in mind that this attraction may not last. Is it worth upsetting everyone and everything for a few moments of passion?

Love: **Friends:**   **Social life:**

OCTOBER 2000

Halloween Horrors

Use your psychic powers (and, yes, we all have them!), and this year's Halloween will be extra spooky!

Note: if any of the technical terms (in italics) used below baffle you, check the glossary on page 213.

As a **Piscean**, you are the dreamer of the zodiac. And that's why many solutions, ideas and messages come to you whilst you're in the dream state (i.e. snoozing).

See page 176 for key to symbols

You're also pretty clairvoyant and are the most likely sign to see a ghost or apparition. If you fancied doing something spooky for a living, you'd make a fab *medium*. (Just be careful not to frighten yourself . . . you're easily spooked!)

Ariens have really good natural instincts: if they get a gut feeling about something, they're usually right. If they want to develop their psychic powers, they should concentrate on seeing into the future. They're also interested in *runes* and *phrenology*. If they were a psychic by trade, they'd be a fortune-teller.

Taureans, like Ariens, should also trust their instincts. Their hidden psychic ability is also *divination*, and they should concentrate on *numerology* and *dowsing* if they want to develop this talent. If they were to choose a psychic career, they'd be *numerologists*.

Geminians are naturally very crafty and clever and can often fool people into believing they're psychic. In actual fact, they are pretty *telepathic* and should use this power wisely. Other areas that may fascinate them are *palmistry* and *graphology*.

Cancerians are highly sensitive and this is a bonus if they're considering developing any psychic talents they might have. If they read up on tea leaf reading and *scrying*, they'd find it very interesting. Their secret psychic talents are *clairaudience* and *clairvoyance*.

Leos have a natural ability to connect with people.

They're good with others on a one-to-one, face-to-face level and have a real interest in other people's lives. They sometimes have great powers of *precognition*, which can be useful. But it's astrology and tarot reading that really enthral a Leo.

Virgoans have extremely sharp intuition, but are rather dubious about the existence of psychic powers. They may not know this, but they actually have a powerful healing touch and would make excellent psychic healers. Next time someone close to them is feeling poorly, they should lay their hands on them and see what happens . . .

Librans are very understanding types and are psychically highly sensitive. Of all the signs, they're the one most likely to possess the ability to see *auras.* If they wanted a psychic career, one as an aura reader would suit them well.

Scorpians are fascinated by all things mysterious and this includes the world of psychic powers. With those amazing eyes and that soft voice, they'd make top hypnotists. Move over, Paul McKenna, and let Miss Scorpio take the stage!

Sagittarians are very open-minded and this can make them psychic in the most dramatic way. Many are *psychokinetic* and some even experience visions. If a Saggie were to choose a psychic career, they'd make a great prophet. (Well, *someone* has to do it . . !)

Capricornians, although quite cynical about psychic stuff, are very tolerant and would never dismiss it as a load of twaddle. What they don't realize is that they're actually pretty psychic; they just don't pay too much attention to that part of themselves, that's all. A career as a colour therapist would suit a Capricorn – it's not too spooky but good intuition is vital. Something they have by the barrowload.

Aquarians are extremely positive and sensitive people and are able to pick up all sorts of signs and signals that others would miss completely. They're interested in what makes other folk tick and would do well studying *biorhythms*. In fact, they could even make a career of it if they wanted . . .

Glossary

Aura = the subtle power that emanates from the body

Biorhythms = body "moods"

Clairaudience = "hearing" voices and/or sounds not perceptible to the other senses

Clairvoyance = the power of seeing or perceiving objects not perceptible to the other senses

Divination = the ability to see into the future

Dowsing = using a divining rod to discover underground water and/or minerals

Graphology = character analysis using handwriting

Medium = someone who can receive information from the "spirit world"

Numerologist = someone who studies the psychic significance of numbers

Numerology = the study of the significance of numbers

Palmistry = studying the hands and palms for character-reading and fortune-telling

Phrenology = character analysis using the bumps on the head!

Precognition = having visions of the future through dreams, ideas, feelings or visions

Psychokinetic = able to move objects without touching them
Runes = carved Scandinavian stones used for fortune-telling
Scrying = crystal ball reading
Telepathic = able to pick up and transmit thoughts without
using the senses of sight, smell, hearing, taste or touch

OCTOBER FORECAST

1st–7th
Mercury in the travel part of your chart predicts an interesting and educational change of scene. This most probably pertains to a school trip: this'll be – fun and will teach you a thing or two too! So don't miss it.

Love: *Friends:* 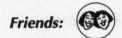 *Social life:*

8th–14th
The Full Moon in your astrological house of cash could see a money problem turning full circle. Whatever financial situation you were in this time last month, it's all changed now. Only you can say if that's a good or bad thing . . .

Love: *Friends:* 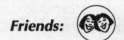 *Social life:*

15th–21st
With gorgeous planet Venus getting cosy in the "power" part of your chart, you should make the most of your looks and charm – these qualities alone could win you big prizes. Add them to your other talents and you can't fail! It's time to make some money too, so squeeze this week for all it's worth!

See page 176 for key to symbols

Love: **Friends:**  **Social life:**

22nd–31st

The Sun in the travel part of your chart forecasts a half-term holiday. Use this time to learn about other people. Oh, and don't forget to have fun too – especially if you're going to any Halloween parties.

Love: **Friends:** **Social life:**

NOVEMBER 2000

Will Your Bonfire Night Go With A Bang?

The only good thing about the dreary month of November is Bonfire Night. Totally agree? Then you must be a Piscean . . .

As a peace- and privacy-loving **Piscean**, you hate noise and crowds: your idea of a nightmare would be a huge public fireworks display. A small party in someone's garden is bad enough, but you'll go if there's a free Lucozade to be had.

Ariens are Fire signs and love a good Bonfire Night. Being ruled by Mars, they're the most likely sign to get burnt (metaphorically or physically) at a bonfire do, so they should be extra vigilant at all times and avoid lighting fireworks. They also get impatient with all the hanging around, and if a party's not well-organized

See page 176 for key to symbols

enough, they may start complaining. Or take over . . .

Taureans quite like Bonfire Night but aren't the biggest socializers in the zodiac. At a fireworks party, Taureans are invariably stood in the shadows, quietly scoffing baked potatoes. Copping off is a rare occurrence: their mouth's too full of grub to snog!!

Geminians *pretend* to like fireworks because fireworks look so cool, but deep down they're petrified of all the whizzing and banging. That's why they always find someone to snog at bonfire parties – they're much happier on a comfy sofa than in a chilly back yard!

Cancerians are always happy to help out at any sort of party, but those of the bonfire variety aren't really their favourites. They prefer edible bangers to the exploding kind and may just turn up for the scoff. And why not indeed . . ?

Leos, as Fire signs, enjoy a good firework display. They're more inclined to attend a big public show than a house party, because they like their fireworks on a grand scale. At-home bonfire "do's" always seem to disappoint them – more so if there's not enough decent totty around . . .

Virgoans are sticklers for everything being just so, so the mess of a bonfire party can really upset them. Whether the party is their own or someone else's, a Virgoan is the "helpful" person hoovering the carpet and sweeping the patio – and, basically, not having very much fun at all.

Librans love the pretty colours of the fireworks and the whole atmosphere of a cracking bonfire party. But, because of the responsibility involved, they're unlikely to throw a party of their own. So they'll just go to other people's and have fun at their expense instead.

Scorpians enjoy bonfire parties – the fireworks, the weather and the fact that it's so close to their birthday sets them aglow with excitement. It can make them feel rather sexy too and more likely than the other signs to cop off with someone.

Sagittarians, as Fire signs, love Guy Fawkes Night. They love parties even more, so the combination of the two is fab! They love getting involved with the setting off of fireworks, but, if there are any sensible people about, Saggies may not be allowed to get their hands on anything dangerous. (They're famous for their carelessness.)

Capricornians reckon that fireworks are dangerous and expensive and, because of this, they're unlikely to ever throw a Bonfire Night party of their own. They may attend someone else's party, but they'll stand well clear of the fireworks and make a lot of tutting noises – much to everyone else's annoyance.

Aquarians think fireworks are an evil waste of money and believe that the cash spent on them every year should be used to buy far more worthy things. They're not overly keen on parties either, so probably wouldn't enjoy a bonfire do too much.

NOVEMBER FORECAST

1st–7th

Mars changes signs on the 4th and brings passion in abundance into your life. If you're in a relationship, something happens which makes you fall in love all over again. If you're single, you won't be for long. Bear in mind that there's a thin line between love and hate – this applies especially when it comes to someone you meet at a fireworks party at the weekend.

Love: *Friends:*   *Social life:*

8th–14th

With Venus in the friends part of your chart, you're in for some fun and mischief. All your worries melt away and your mates (Taurean and Libran ones in particular) are extra supportive. Hurrah!

Love: *Friends:*   *Social life:*

15th–21st

The Full Moon in the communications part of your chart means you shouldn't cling on to a certain person or situation just because you know it's safe. You know that changes need to be made and, scary though that might be, it has to be done. You should receive some news this week which will reinforce this message. Don't ignore it: getting that particular news at this particular time is no coincidence . . .

Love: *Friends:*    *Social life:*

See page 176 for key to symbols

22nd–30th

The Sun changes signs and makes you extra strong and determined. You may be tempted to fake it in some way this week (it could make your life so much easier), but the planets advise you to be yourself at all times. Any kind of pretence will soon backfire on you and ruin your plans. So be real!

Love: **Friends:**   **Social life:**

DECEMBER 2000

Cosmic Christmas Gifts

Because, astrologically speaking, the outer and inner self are often totally different, what we want and what we actually get for Christmas are equally different. If you're wondering what gifts to buy your friends and family this year, read this first . . .

As a dainty, romantic and nostalgic **Piscean**, you always get very elegant presents: perfume, original 1940s negligees and silk scarves mainly. But, unbeknown to many, you're actually pretty gauche and would be much happier with a pair of silly sunglasses and a weird wig. (Oh, and don't forget the funny fart cushion!)

Ariens are secretly rather glam, but because very few people actually realize this, they're likely to get something very practical for Christmas. They wish their

See page 176 for key to symbols

friends and family would stop buying them sensible slippers and handy tool kits, and would splash out on some gorgeously sexy and frivolous undies instead.

Taureans are viewed as couldn't-care-less types, so people rarely put much thought into gifts for them. But Taureans are actually quite snooty, so anything cheap 'n' nasty *won't* be well received. In fact, the average Taurean would rather have nothing than something that isn't of the highest quality. So there you have it . . . Nothing it is!

Geminians, although cutely kitsch on the surface, are actually – on the sneak – a bit of a class act. They'd be eternally grateful for a nice pair of suede gloves. But what do they get? Fluffy mules and a feather boa – that's what! Ta very much, Santa . . .

Cancerians are modest types who don't ask for much. Yeah – right! Like they'd be happy with a set of hankies or a nice book! Forget it! Underneath that "no-really-I-just-don't-need-anything" exterior, lies a total pressie-grabber – the more the merrier as far as they're concerned.

Leos love very expensive, quality gifts. Simple, eh? So why does everyone insist on buying them such a load of old tack every Christmas? All they want is a nice little something in white gold or platinum, but no. Mates and Santa alike come bearing gifts of the see-thru' nightie, nasty perfume and cheap chocs variety instead.

Virgoans may seem shy, but beneath that slightly inhibited surface lies a complete wild child. Ask a Virgoan what they really want for Christmas and you may well be shocked by their answer. But a gnome hat and matching scarf is about as shocking as the pressies ever get. Sad but true . . .

Librans, although quite fluffy on the surface, would love nothing more than a nice pair of thermal long-johns. So why do friends and relatives shower them with exotic lingerie year in year out? OK, so they may look fab in a satin g-string, but they'd much rather have something for everyday wear.

Scorpians are fed up with all the black tights and socks people throw their way every Christmas. It's not that they don't use them, it's just most Scorpians have at least 150 pairs! Cheer them up this year by buying them some nice pink ones instead. It's this year's black anyway (maybe . . .)!

Sagittarians are always given outdoory, sporty clothes as pressies. Football shirts, anything in their fave teams' colours and big woolly jumpers. But all they really want is a bit of '70s glam. So go to town (steering well clear of Millets of course) and bring 'em back a glittery acrylic cardi and a pair of crimplene hot pants!

Capricornians, notorious for their dislike of extravagance, are always "treated" to cheap 'n' cheerful gifts – shoelaces, a nice egg cup, a manicure set . . . Secretly though, they'd rather have something hideously expensive: in fact, anything that costs less than £1000, as far as they're concerned, is barely worth a thank-you note.

Aquarians, outwardly sane but inwardly mad as hatters, are often disappointed to find clothing made of tweed, itchy wool and corduroy in their Christmas stocking. If only people realized how much happier they'd be with some glittery nail polish, false eyelashes and an "I'm With Stupid" T-shirt!

DECEMBER FORECAST

1st–7th

When Mercury changes signs on the 4th, your attention turns to school. You know what you're capable of, so why don't you stretch yourself and prove it? If school's a bore, talk to a teacher and see if they can offer any solutions.

Love: ♡   *Friends:*   *Social life:*

8th–14th

Venus makes a transit and marks the start of a new phase in your love-life. Trouble is, this could be the beginning of a destination-nowhere fling, in that the guy of your dreams happens to be totally unavailable or totally unsuitable. Keeping secrets and/or telling lies are badly starred right now. If in doubt, get the advice of your mum. And listen to what she has to say this time . . .

See page 176 for key to symbols

Love: **Friends:** 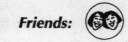   **Social life:**

15th–21st

As the Sun prepares to change signs, you're in hot demand with your mates and the boys, so this weekend is a great time to party. Meeting new people and taking on new hobbies are well starred too. So go for it! You won't be disappointed.

Love: **Friends:** 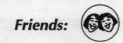   **Social life:**

22nd–31st

Mercury in the friends part of your chart causes you to ask whether certain mates really have your interests at heart. It also makes you question whether you really have the same beliefs as your mates: if you haven't, why do you pretend you have? Mars changes signs on Xmas Eve and advises you not to be overcautious with regards to a certain project. Now's the time to be fearless and strong. With the Xmas Day New Moon in the social part of your chart, you don't intend to get involved with anything you might consider dull. (Lucky it's Xmas then really, isn't it?) Planning for the future excites you this week, so make some really positive New Year resolutions . . .

Love: **Friends:**    **Social life:**

See page 176 for key to symbols

Part 11:

Into The New Millennium!

What does the first part of the new millennium hold for you? How are you and your life going to change in the next decade? To find out the answers to these and a whole load more questions, check out our Ten-Year Forecast . . .

Soul-Searching And Psychic Powers!

The eclipse on January 9th makes it ultra-important for you to get to know yourself and to understand your needs. You want to be happy but to get to that state you need to examine yourself mentally, emotionally and spiritually. Until you know yourself, you won't know what you really need. So get soul-searching!

If you're keen to make some major changes this year, make them before mid-March or after mid-August, as Pluto is going backwards between these dates and could cause problems for you. Transforming your life will be a whole lot easier after August.

At the end of October, a transiting Mars warns you to keep jealous feelings under wraps, or certain friendships could end in tears.

After a period of retrograde motion, your ruler Neptune starts going forwards in October, making this the most magical time. It's a very romantic time for you too, but with Neptune, being a rather nebulous planet, it's never very clear what's going to happen next, indicating perhaps that it'll be Fate – not you – that affects the outcome. Mars in your sign from December 9th gives you the strength and determination to do well, and this could go towards triggering a change in your life. This could be quite subtle, so don't expect any great dramas. Christmas will be a quiet affair.

A Thin Line . . .

With Pluto following a similar pattern to last year, everything pertaining to your future plans could be a bit of a rollercoaster between March and August.

Lusty Mars is in the passion part of your chart from mid-October and this will have a memorable effect in the romance department – in fact, your love life will be pretty intense. That's not to say it'll be easy . . . There are problems a-plenty due to the fact that someone's being selfish. (Surely it can't be you!) If you want things to work out, you need to start thinking and behaving as part of a couple. Cooperation and compromise are the answers. Remember though – there's a thin line between love and hate and around this time you could be discovering just how true that old saying is . . .

The eclipse on December 4th distracts you from all the festivities, and there could be problems with regards to your plans for the future. You suddenly realize that you're on the wrong track and could go about getting on the right one.

Things will be occupying your mind somewhat and you probably won't even notice Xmas as it comes and goes . . .

Secrets, Lies And Growing Up

2003

As Mercury transits three signs in March, you're all over the place, scattering your energy here, there and everywhere. Writing is extremely well starred after the 5th, so whether you're writing to your old Auntie, or entering a short story competition, whatever comes out of your pen will be pure genius! So get scribbling!

Mars remains in the "secrets" part of your chart throughout May, making life a bit weird. One so-called mate doesn't seem to like you very much and seems to be doing everything in his/her power to muck things up for you. All you can do is give this unpleasant individual a wide berth and try your hardest to ignore what they're doing. Rest assured, they'll soon see the error of their ways. The position of Jupiter from the end of August bodes well for close friendships and relationships with the opposite sex.

November's second eclipse on the 23rd means you could be reviewing your career plans. There's a good chance of you completely changing direction around this time, but certain practicalities may get in the way of you putting your new plans into action.

In December, Mars in the cash part of your chart bodes well for any moneymaking ideas you might have. Just in time for a Xmas spree!

Life In The Fast Lane

2004

Jupiter starts going backwards through your opposite sign on January 3rd. Friendships made during this time could be rather superficial, so enjoy them over the New Year but don't expect them to last . . .

Venus in your sign from January 15th makes for a pleasant and relaxing time. In February, Mars enters the communications part of your chart and you start to experience life in the fast lane; around this time, you could make crucial decisions that alter your life quite radically. Everything seems to be happening so quickly – just the way you like it!

Jolly Jupiter starts moving forwards in May and your life changes for the better. You could start a new romance this month and what a laugh that'll be, as you and your new paramour discover that you share more than just a sense of humour.

At the end of July, as Mercury enters your opposite sign, you're advised that the best way to solve problems of the romantic kind is through talking. Keeping your feelings bottled up, although seemingly a good idea initially, won't help you or your bloke ultimately.

A transiting Mars makes you a proper little love-magnet in September. You're in for a lusty time (more so if you're holidaying) – and it's not just the weather that'll be hot, hot, hot! This makes autumn a whole lot of fun – and Xmas will be even better!

Living Dangerously  2005

For most of April, you should keep a tight rein on your spending – you're chucking money around like it's confetti. Work out what's going on and get a grip! (The Sun and Venus in the money part of your chart don't help, so you'll have to make an extra-huge effort.)

In May, with Mars in your sign, you're feeling much more on top of things – in fact, you're coming across as thoroughly assertive and dynamic. This is the time for doing great things, and as long as you're quick to put your ideas into action, you will be in for some good luck and destined for BIG success. Hurry up though – your ruler Neptune changes direction in mid-May and this will be one of those times that you lose a bit of your natural Piscean sparkle.

As energetic Mars leaves your sign on June 12th, you'll have some excellent money-making ideas. Get things off the ground quickly – it's the early bird that catches the worm, remember?

The Mars transit in October means that although you want to take risks and live dangerously, you can't quite bring yourself to do it. Xmas will be a good time to sort out some of your better ideas from the not so clever . . .

Making Improvements . . .

Mercury in Pisces from February 9th makes you feel a bit restless. It's a good time to promote yourself though – tell others just how fabulous you are! – and move forwards in every area.

In June, Mars moves into the work part of your chart, indicating that if you're feeling fed up with the sheer tedium of your everyday life (and it might well be a bit routine around this time), then worry no more, as certain opportunities enable you to make improvements both to your working environment and to your relationships with your individual work colleagues.

In July, Mars in your opposite sign forecasts arguments between you and someone you're very close to. There's a lot of selfishness going on and this needs to be sorted – unless you *want* the relationship to collapse, that is . . .

From August, holidays are well starred and a holiday romance is a strong possibility. Venus enters the work part of your chart in mid-August and this doesn't exactly make it easy for you to get things done.

A transiting Venus on November 17th bodes well for work – in fact, you could be in for a big promotion. Don't underestimate the power of your sex appeal this month – it could get you just what you've always wanted, and a whole lot more.

A Brilliant Birthday And Learning To Look Good

As Venus changes signs on February 21st, you may come to a realization about your spending habits and this'll affect your destiny in one way or another. Venus puts you in a lovely mood throughout March – now's a good time for parties (your own birthday do will be particularly enjoyable – not to mention eventful).

This year, you seem to be putting a lot of your energy into improving your image, as you realize how looking good is imperative to your ultimate personal success.

The total eclipse in your opposite sign on March 3rd indicates big changes with regards to your love life.

In July, Venus links love to travel. If you're spending any time away from home, you could be in for a romantic treat!

A retrograde Saturn in your opposite sign from December 19th forecasts a crisis in a close friendship or romance. Why are you feeling so guilty all the time? Make an effort to say what you want and the relationship should improve. This transit also forecasts a sudden lack of enthusiasm in all your closest relationships. If you're looking for true love, you may have to wait – at least until after Xmas.

A Very Special Year

2008

This year, you're not only destined for several big changes, but to relearn a few hard facts of life. Pluto, the planet of transformation, last changed signs back in 1995 but now, as the New Year dawns, it's ready to make a move again. This could be a rather turbulent time for you, especially if you find yourself in a dilemma about your long-term plans. You're a big believer in Fate at the best of times, and should feel comfortable about being carried along by Destiny for a while. There's not much you can do to alter things, so you may as well just go with the flow.

This major transit also means that the year 2008 will be a very memorable one for you – if you play your cards right and remain positive.

The eclipse in your opposite sign on February 21st advises you to face up to any problems you might be having in your most intimate relationship.

Saturn changes direction in your opposite sign in May and puts your closest relationship under the microscope. If you've been having problems, now's the time to patch things up.

In November, Neptune starts moving forwards, giving you back some of the sparkle and confidence you may have been lacking lately. You're at your most intuitive, and should use this to further your own interests from now until the end of the year.

Making Money And Changing Direction

As Jupiter changes signs in January, you realize that someone's got it in for you. OK, so you can be paranoid at the best of times, but this time it's for real. Avoid anyone you think might be jealous or envious of you or yours. Try not to do anything devious: it's bad karma.

As Mars leaves your sign on April 23rd, your attention turns to making money.

In September, Pluto changes direction, which means your destiny becomes linked to a friend's: wherever one of you goes, the other is sure to follow . . .

Venus makes October a really special time for you: if there are any love problems to be dealt with though, deal with them. Certain stuff may be hard to talk about but talking's the only way to work things out.

Saturn changes signs on the penultimate day of October, and this interferes with your love life. Saturn transits are always a bit tricky because Saturn's such a serious planet. Here, it advises you to work out why you're feeling the way you're feeling. Pretending everything's OK when it's clearly *not* OK isn't going to get you anywhere. If you don't like the way things are going, alter your plans. Do something completely different if that's what you fancy. By the end of the year, you're feeling a lot more positive.

Older And Wiser

In January, Saturn moves backwards in the passion part of your chart. If you're bored with your love-life, don't panic. Stay calm and all will turn out OK. As Jupiter enters Pisces on January 13th, you enter a brilliant – and lucky – chapter of your life.

At the end of April, as Venus changes signs, family fun is forecast, with parties galore. In May, as Uranus enters the money part of your chart, cash matters get quite chaotic. Around this time, you'll either come into some dosh or lose everything you've ever managed to save. Whatever happens, it's all part of Uranus's plan to get you moving onwards and upwards.

You're feeling hot throughout the summer – and that's not just down to the weather! You're so sexy that you're totally irresistible. Use your charms wisely – there is such a thing as too many boyfriends, you know!

In September, Jupiter moves backwards into your sign and could cause problems: you're supposed to be maturing, not regressing, so what's going on?

The eclipse in the domestic part of your chart on December 21st means it may be harder than you expect to solve family problems, but things will be OK if you communicate with each other Then you can get ready for a happy family Xmas.

At the end of the decade, you're not only ten years older – you're ten years wiser too!

Part 12:

Birthday Chart

Not sure which friend is which star sign? Need an at-a-glance reminder of all your mates' birthdays? Want to know which celeb shares your date of birth? Then fill in this specially devised (starting with Aries and ending with Pisces) birthday chart and fret no more . . .

ARIES

March

20 _____

21 Mark Hamilton (Ash), 1977; Ario (N'Tyce), 1974

22 _____

23 Damon Albarn (Blur), 1968; Marti Pellow, 1966

24 _____

25 Elton John, 1947; Mel (All Saints), 1975

26 _____

27 Mariah Carey, 1969

28 _____

29 Coree (Damage), 1978

30 Celine Dion, 1968

31 _____

April

1 Chris Evans and Jean Claude Van Damme, 1966; Phillip Schofield, 1962

2 Linford Christie, 1960

3 Will Mellor, 1976

4 Robert Downey Jnr, 1965

5 _____

6 Chantal (N-Tyce), 1977

7 Victoria Adams, 1975

8

9

10

11   Cerys Matthews, 1966

12   Paul Nicholls, 1979

13

14

15

16

17

18

19

TAURUS

20   Luther Vandross, 1951

21   The Queen, 1926

22

23

24   Jas Mann (Babylon Zoo), 1971

25

26

27

28

29   Michelle Pfeiffer, 1958

30

May

1   Joanna Lumley, 1947

2

Birthday Chart

3 Jay Darlington (Kula Shaker), 1969

4

5

6

7

8 Dave Rowntree (Blur), 1964

9

10 Bono (U2), 1960

11 Harry Enfield, 1961

12 Emilio Estevez, 1962

13

14 Sinead (B*Witched), 1978; Nat (All Saints), 1973

15

16 Janet Jackson, 1966

17

18

19

20 Sean Conlon (5ive), 1981; Cher, 1946

GEMINI

21

22 Naomi Campbell, 1970

23

24

25

26 Lenny Kravitz, 1964

27 Paul Gascoigne, 1964; Denise Van Outen, 1974

28 Kylie Minogue, 1968

29 Adam Rickitt, 1978; Noel Gallagher, 1967; Mel B, 1975

30 Sally Whittaker (Coronation Street), 1963

31

June

1

2

3

4 Noah Wyle, 1971

5

6

7 Prince, 1958

8 Mick Hucknall, 1960

9 Johnny Depp, 1963; Michael J. Fox, 1961

10 Liz Hurley, 1965

11

12

13 Jason Brown (5ive), 1976

14 Boy George, 1961

15 Courtney Cox, 1967

16

17

18 Paul McCartney, 1942

19

20 Nicole Kidman, 1966

CANCER

21 Prince William, 1982

22

23

24

25 Jamie Redknapp, 1973; George Michael, 1963

26

27

28 Adam Woodyatt (Ian Beale in EastEnders), 1969

29 Richard Abindin Breen (5ive), 1979

30

July

1 Keith Duffy (Boyzone), 1974; Pamela Anderson, 1967

2

3 Shane Lynch (Boyzone), 1976; Tom Cruise, 1962

4

5

6 Sylvester Stallone, 1946

7

8

9 Tom Hanks, 1956

10 Neil Tennant (Pet Shop Boys), 1954

11 Richie Sambora (Bon Jovi), 1960

12 Anna Friel, 1976

13 Harrison Ford, 1947

14

15

16

17

18

19 Anthony Edwards (ER), 1962

20

21 Ross Kemp (EastEnders), 1964; Robin Williams, 1952

22

LEO

23 _____

24 _____

25 Matt Le Blanc, 1967 _____

26 _____

27 _____

28 _____

29 _____

30 Sean Moore (Manic Street Preachers), 1970; Arnold Schwarzenegger, 1947

31 Fatboy Slim, 1963 _____

August

1 _____

2 _____

3 _____

4 _____

5 _____

6 Geri Halliwell, 1972; Barbara Windsor (Peggy in EastEnders), 1937

7 David Duchovny, 1960 _____

8 _____

9 Whitney Houston, 1963 _____

10 _____

11 Andrez (Damage), 1978 _____

12 _____

13 _____

14 Halle Berry, 1968 _____

15 Mikey Graham, 1972 (Boyzone); Spike (911), 1974

16 Madonna, 1958 _____

17 Robert de Niro, 1943 _____

18 Christian Slater, 1969; Patrick Swayze, 1952

19

20

21   Dina Carroll, 1968

22   Howard Dwayne Dorough (Backstreet Boys), 1973

VIRGO

23   Richard Neville (5ive), 1979; Shaun Ryder, 1962

24   Stephen Fry, 1957

25   Elvis Costello, 1958

26   Macaulay Culkin, 1980

27

28

29   Michael Jackson, 1958

30

31   Richard Gere, 1949

September

1   Gloria Estefan, 1957

2   Keanu Reeves, 1965

3   Charlie Sheen, 1965

4   Kevin Kennedy (Coronation Street), 1961

5

6

7

8

9   Hugh Grant, 1960

10

11

12

13

14

15

16

17

18
---
19 Jarvis Cocker, 1966; Paul Winterhart (Kula Shaker), 1971

20
---
21 Liam Gallagher, 1972; Jimmy Constable (911), 1973

22

LIBRA

23

24
---
25 Declan Donnelly, 1977; Will Smith, 1968

26
---
27 Lee Anthony Brennan (911), 1975

28
---
29 Brett Anderson (Suede), 1967

30

October

1
---
2 Sting, 1952
---
3 Kevin Scott Richardson (Backstreet Boys), 1972
---
4 Alicia Silverstone, 1976
---
5 Kate Winslet, 1975

6

7 Michelle (N-Tyce), 1974

8

9

10

11 Dawn French, 1957

12

13

14 Shaznay (All Saints), 1975; Cliff Richard, 1940

15

16

17

18

19

20 Dannii Minogue, 1970

21 Donna (N-Tyce), 1976

22 Jeff Goldblum, 1952; Zac Hanson, 1985

SCORPIO

23

24 Alonza Bevan (Kula Shaker), 1970

25

26

27

28 Joaquin Phoenix, 1977; Julia Roberts, 1967

29 Winona Ryder, 1971

30

31

November

1
_____

2
_____

3 Ras (Damage), 1976; Roseanne, 1952
_____

4 Kavanna, 1977; Louise Nurding, 1974
_____

5 Bryan Adams, 1959
_____

6 Ethan Hawke, 1970
_____

7
_____

8
_____

9
_____

10
_____

11 Leonardo DiCaprio, 1974; Demi Moore, 1962
_____

12 David Schwimmer, 1966
_____

13 Whoopi Goldberg, 1955
_____

14 Prince Charles, 1948; Usher, 1978
_____

15
_____

16
_____

17 Jonathan Ross, 1960; Ike Hanson, 1980
_____

18 Ant McPartlin , 1975
_____

19 Meg Ryan, 1961; Jodie Foster, 1962
_____

20
_____

21 Alex James (Blur), 1968
_____

22 Scott Robinson (5ive), 1979
_____

SAGITTARIUS

23 Zoe Ball, 1970
_____

24
_____

25
_____

Birthday Chart

26   Tina Turner, 1939

27

28   Dane (Another Level), 1979

29   Ryan Giggs, 1973

30   Gary Lineker, 1960

December

1

2

3

4

5

6

7   Aaron Carter, 1987; Nic (All Saints), 1974

8   Kim Basinger, 1953; Sinead O'Connor, 1966

9

10

11

12

13

14   Michael Owen, 1979

15   Adele & Keavey (B*Witched), 1979

16

17

18   Lindsay (B*Witched), 1980; Brad Pitt, 1965; Robson Green, 1964; Stephen Spielberg, 1947

19

20

21   Jamie Theakston, 1970

CAPRICORN

22 Noel Edmonds, 1948

23

24

25

26 Jared Leto, 1969

27

28 Denzel Washington, 1954

29

30

31 Val Kilmer, 1959

January

1 Noel (Damage), 1976

2

3 Mel Gibson, 1956

4 Tim (Ash), 1977; Beth Gibbons (Portishead), 1965; Michael Stipe (REM), 1960

5

6 Rowan Atkinson, 1956

7

8 David Bowie, 1947; Karen Poole (Alisha's Attic), 1971

9 AJ (Backstreet Boys), 1978

10 Rod Stewart, 1945

11

12 Mel C, 1976

13

14

15

16 Kate Moss, 1974

17 Jim Carrey, 1962

18 Kevin Costner, 1955; Crispian Mills (Kula Shaker), 1973

19

20 Gary Barlow, 1971

AQUARIUS

21 Emma Bunton, 1976

22

23

24 Vic Reeves, 1959

25

26

27 Mark Owen, 1974

28 Nick Carter (Backstreet Boys), 1980; Elijah Wood, 1981

29

30

31

February

1

2

3

4 Natalie Imbruglia, 1975

5 Bobby Brown, 1969

6

7 Axl Rose (Guns 'n' Roses), 1962; Danny Goffey (Supergrass), 1974

8

9

10

11 Brandy (Jennifer Brandy Norwood), 1979

12 Jade Jones (Damage), 1979

13 Robbie Williams, 1974

14

15

16

17

18 Matt Dillon, 1964; John Travolta, 1954

PISCES

19

20 Ian Brown (Stone Roses), 1963; Cindy Crawford, 1966

21 James Bradfield (Manic Street Preachers), 1969

22

23 Drew Barrymore, 1975

24

25

26

27 Peter Andre, 1973

28

29

March

1

2 Jon Bon Jovi, 1962

3 Ronan Keating (Boyzone), 1977

4 Evan Dando, 1967; Patsy Kensit, 1968

5

6 Shaquille O'Neal, 1972

Birthday Chart

7

8

9

10 Neneh Cherry, 1964

11

12 Graham Coxon (Blur), 1969; Kelly Bryan (Eternal), 1975

13 Adam Clayton (U2), 1960

14 Taylor Hanson, 1983

15

16 Jimmy Nail, 1954

17 Stephen Gately (Boyzone), 1976

18

19 Bruce Willis, 1955